Praise for *FedTelligence*

With the consolidation or elimination of servicing human resources offices, any federal employee—from those who are new to Uncle Sam's civilian army to those nearing retirement—will benefit from Ann Vanderslice's insight and knowledge of the federal workforce and human resources system. Your financial security depends in large part on understanding how the federal HR system works. *FedTelligence – The Ultimate Guide to Mastering Your Federal Benefits* will help any reader understand and use this complex system.

Ralph Smith
CEO, FedSmith.com

Ann Vanderslice is one of the most respected and knowledgeable federal benefits trainers and financial planners in the industry. Now through *FedTelligence*, any federal employee can reap the benefit of her experience as she clearly articulates the complexities of federal retirement benefits in this comprehensive guidebook. *FedTelligence* is a must read for all federal employees that want to make the most of their financial resources in retirement.

Gay Page
Executive Director, Colorado Federal Executive Board

FedTelligence gives you a wealth of information on how to maximize the federal benefit package. Ann greatly simplifies this complex topic and her sincerity towards helping federal employees really shines through in the many "real-life" examples found in this must-read book.

Kevin Hocker
Two-time award-winning author of *The Success Compass*

Ann Vanderslice has written a comprehensive guide to federal benefits. Taking into account all the complexities from retirement to the Thrift Savings Plan to insurance benefits, she makes the process clear and understandable. With the most current and accurate information available, this book will help design your blueprint for retirement. *FedTelligence* is a valuable tool for any federal employee.

Mary Beth Saldin
Former Director Veteran's Health Administration—Retired

Ann Vanderslice understands what it takes for a federal employee to plan for retirement, both financially and from a benefits perspective. Her extensive work with an almost exclusive federal client base makes her uniquely qualified to help feds plan for a secure retirement. This book is loaded with information and entertaining examples that are relevant to many federal employees who are contemplating their retirement. I recommend this for federal employees at all stages of retirement planning.

Tammy Flanagan
Senior Benefits Director, National Institute of Transition Planning, Inc.

FedTelligence

FedTelligence

The **Ultimate** Guide to
Mastering Your Federal Benefits
(Your Declaration of Independence)

Ann Vanderslice

Published by Advantage, Charleston, South Carolina.
Member of Advantage Media Group.

ADVANTAGE is a registered trademark and the Advantage colophon is a trademark of Advantage Media Group, Inc.

Printed in the United States of America.

ISBN: 978-159932-296-4
LCCN: 2012930888

This publication is designed to provide accurate and authoritative information in regard to the subject matter covered. It is sold with the understanding that the publisher is not engaged in rendering legal, accounting, or other professional services. If legal advice or other expert assistance is required, the services of a competent professional person should be sought.

Tree Neutral

Advantage Media Group is proud to be a part of the Tree Neutral® program. Tree Neutral offsets the number of trees consumed in the production and printing of this book by taking proactive steps such as planting trees in direct proportion to the number of trees used to print books. To learn more about Tree Neutral, please visit **www.treeneutral.com**. To learn more about Advantage's commitment to being a responsible steward of the environment, please visit **www.advantagefamily.com/green**

Advantage Media Group is a leading publisher of business, motivation, and self-help authors. Do you have a manuscript or book idea that you would like to have considered for publication? Please visit **www.amgbook.com** or call **1.866.775.1696**

TABLE OF CONTENTS

Introduction

Fedtelligence *(fed-'tel-lə-jən[t]s)* derived from the Latin verb *intellegere*

1. A very general mental capability around the benefits of the federal government that involves the ability to reason, plan, solve problems, think abstractly, comprehend complex ideas, learn quickly and learn from experience.

2. "Intelligence" (understanding) is different from being "smart" (capable of adapting to the environment).

3. Mastery of available federal benefits and utilization of those benefits to your advantage.

What if the retirement finish line turns out to be a cliff?

Carmen had retired from the Bureau of Land Management at age 56, as soon as she'd celebrated 30 years of working for the government. Each day she sent her husband off to work and, on this particular Tuesday, she had just settled into her morning routine with her second cup of coffee and the paper when the phone rang. The caller ID told her that it was Jerry, her former supervisor, on the line. After a few minutes of chitchat on the wonders of retirement, Jerry said, "Carmen, I have some news for you. We've received notification from OPM that you are six months short of being eligible to retire."

Carmen's heart sank. Her worst nightmare was coming true — she wasn't actually retired! Jerry went on, "The good news, if there is such a thing in this situation, is that your old position hasn't been filled. You can come back and complete the time you need to qualify for retirement."

In the back of every retiree's mind is the nagging worry that they've missed something, that their retirement won't go as expected, that they've neglected to fill out some form. This book is designed to ease those fears and make sure you aren't afraid to answer the phone once you've retired.

Carmen's story had a happy ending – if you call being able to go back to her job to complete her 30 years a happy ending. What if Carmen's job had already been filled? What if she had already moved out of state to a new retirement home? What if Jerry had already retired and there hadn't been anyone to advocate for Carmen?

FedTelligence is about not only making sure you haven't missed anything – it's about making the most of your benefits along the way. By understanding how your benefit package fits together, you'll create a strategy that works while you're working and once you're retired.

Retirement for federal employees is a very complex system, and it can feel a bit overwhelming to deal with when you're working every day. You probably made some of your benefit elections years ago, and you haven't thought about them since then. Now, it seems as if there are all these new choices and elections that you must make. And these decisions can feel as if they're irreversible; if you make a mistake, there's no going back.

There are a lot of options to consider. The purpose of this book is to walk you through some of the pitfalls that can come up, review some of the things that you should expect, help you to control the things that you can control, and learn to live with the rest.

After 20 years working in corporate America, I went into financial services in 2000. Two years into that career, I literally fell into working with federal employees, because of a long-term care open season for federal employees. That was my expertise – where I started in financial services – and it seemed to me that putting a group of federal employees in a conference room and providing a webinar wasn't the best approach. That was 2002 and I never looked back. I've been working with federal employees exclusively ever since.

Even as someone who is considered one of the foremost experts in the country on federal benefits, it takes continuous effort to keep up with legislative proposals and changes and to help those with very complicated employment situations manage their retirement.

My profession as a federal benefits specialist is to help you navigate your way safely to retirement, and to let you know what to expect along the way. There are some things that are out of your control, and you might as well let go of those. But there are a lot of things that you can control and by doing certain things right and checking certain boxes correctly, we can make that trip a little smoother. My role throughout this book is to act as your guide, pointing out not only possible speed bumps, but also opportunities that you have to make the most of your extensive benefits.

This book is intentionally small in size to avoid being threatening. (The benefits provide the intimidation!) It is designed so that you can refer easily to whatever chapter is applicable to your particular situation, without having to read and digest the entire book. I hope you'll use FedTelligence as a guide to navigate your way to peaceful days and restful nights.

Calculating Your Future—CSRS and FERS

*"I would not give a fig for the simplicity this side
of complexity, but I would give my life for the
simplicity on the other side of complexity."*

Oliver Wendell Holmes

The answer to most complicated problems often turns out to be ridiculously simple. But in order to see and understand the simple answers, we must first wade through what seems like overwhelming complexities in order to organize, prioritize, and unify them so that simple solutions can emerge.

As a federal employee, you are a part of the largest workforce in the country, currently about 2.7 million federal employees. You have a complicated set of benefits. You may have started your career under the original retirement system known as the Civil Service Retirement System, or CSRS, which began in 1920. The first person who retired from that system did so in 1926. After the initial rush to retirement (about 5,000 people retired within the first 2 months – some of whom were more than 90 years old!), the next people to retire from that system did so in 1926. When they calculated their benefits, they did it with a pencil and paper – and they still calculate your benefits that same way today. The Office of Personnel Management, OPM, has made three attempts at automating the system (the last attempt inappropriately named Retire EZ), but they've never been able to accomplish it. That tells you a little bit about how complicated the benefits are.

If you came to work for the federal government before January 1st of 1984, you are most likely in CSRS, which has its own unique set of characteristics. If you were hired after January 1st of 1984, you were required to pay into Social Security, and a brand-new government pension system was created called the Federal Employees Retirement System or FERS.

CHAPTER ONE

CSRS – The Extinction of *Fedasaurus Rex*

L ess than 15% of the current federal workforce is made up of CSRS participants. The Office of Personnel Management projects that by 2019, all participants in the older of the two retirement systems will be retired or at least eligible to retire. This leads to the inevitable extinction of another species, not unlike the dinosaur, the *Fedasaurus Rex.*

Mary started as a GS 1 with USDA while she was still in high school. She'll finish her career as a GS 15. After starting in the mailroom, Mary now has responsibility for a multi-million dollar budget and manages a large staff. What an amazing career path! She had many mentors along the way who helped her progression, but ultimately, it was her work ethic and willingness to learn that propelled her to the top. There are numerous stories like Mary's of hardworking individuals who've made public service their life's work.

It's popular in the press these days to bash federal employees. Headlines proclaim that the average federal worker makes twice as much as a private sector worker, that federal employee benefits are better than the private sector employees, and that federal retiree payments are unsustainable.

It's easy to generalize and take shots at federal employees as a group. But the truth is that Mary and others like her have spent their entire careers in public service and made sacrifices to do so. For the 400,000 or so current CSRS employees and all those who came before them – if no one else has told you lately, thank you for your public service.

In CSRS, two components are used to calculate a pension or annuity. (These terms refer to the guaranteed monthly amount you'll receive for the rest of your life.) First, you have to be eligible to retire, which is based on the combination of your age and your years of federal service.

To be eligible, you have to be at least 55 years old and have worked for the government for 30 years. Or, you can be 60 years old and have 20 years of service; or you can be 62 years old and have 5 years of service.

Most of the people in the two latter groups have already retired, so we're addressing those who are in their 50s, the majority of whom already have 30 years of service. Once you're at least 55 years old, and have at least 30 years of service, you're in what I call the Three Bad Days Club, because now you're eligible to retire on an immediate annuity that gets paid out to you on a monthly basis for the rest of your life. We joke that if you have three bad days in a row at work, you're gone. That's how you decide when to retire.

The Civil Service Retirement System is under attack right now, along with other federal employee benefits. Congress and the general public seem to think that if we just had a smaller government and fewer federal employees, all of our problems would be solved. Of course, when we start to put a pencil to paper we know this isn't true but, as I write this, there's a lot of talk about changing the benefits structure. I can only tell you how it works today, of course, but the threat of those benefits changing is causing federal employees to retire in significantly higher numbers than we've seen in the past few years. In an average year, about 57,000 federal employees retire. That number is up about 58% so far in 2011.

Once you are eligible to retire, the first question is, "What's the best day to retire? There must be some way that I can figure out how to make the most of my benefits and pick the one best day of the year."

Let me just say that your best day to retire is when you are eligible and you decide you want to go. Beyond that, if you want to utilize sick and annual leave, here's some advice on how best to do just that.

The best day to retire under the Civil Service Retirement System is either on the last day of the month, or in the first three days of a new month. Most CSRS employees choose to retire on the third of the month, because they get paid their salary (which is higher than their pension will be) through the third, and then they start getting their pensions on the fourth day of the month. They have no unpaid days, and they've maximized the most of their salary. If you can combine that third day of the month with the end of a pay period, you're going to accrue eight more hours of annual leave and four more hours of sick leave.

About 70% of CSRS employees choose to retire at the end of the year, because it may also be the end of a pay period and the end of the annual leave year, where you can roll over 240 hours of annual leave. In addition, if you don't take any of your annual leave for your final year of work, you can actually take 208 hours of accrued leave that you didn't use in that last year before retiring, and get paid for that in a lump sum.

Retiring CSRS employees can be paid out a maximum total of 448 hours of annual leave (240 are carryover and 208 are maximum one-year annual accrual). That leave gets paid out in the new year, and goes onto the next year's tax return. If there's a cost of living adjustment for that year, you get the COLA (cost of living adjustments) on that lump sum annual leave. It's a win-win-win situation, which is why the majority choose to retire at the end of the year. The best dates for retirement for 2012 are:

CSRS

- February 1, 2 or 3
- March 1 or 2
- April 2 or 3
- May 1, 2 or 3
- June 1 (also end of pay period)
- July 2 or 3
- August 1, 2 or 3
- September 3 (also holiday)
- October 1, 2 or 3
- November 1 or 2 (also end of pay period)

- December 3

- January 1, 2 or 3, 2013

Planning to retire sometime after 2012? Here's a link to the best dates to retire from now through 2020!

www.annvanderslice.com/best-dates-to-retire/

Documents You'll Need To Have:

One of the key things I'd encourage you to do, right now, is to create a file folder for yourself that says "Retirement Documents" on it. Don't wait until you need them; it's much easier to take care of these now, before you're filling out your retirement paperwork. Here's what you need to have inside your folder:

- A certified copy of your birth certificate. When you go to apply for Medicare, they're going to expect you to prove you're 65, as will Social Security if you're eligible.

- If you were in the military, you'll need your discharge form, the DD214, because you may be able to count the time you served in the military towards your federal service, depending on when that service occurred and whether you've made a deposit for this service.

- A copy of your Social Security statement, which says how many quarters you've worked. You have to go online (Visit www.ssa.gov/estimator) to look at your estimated benefits, and you can print it out from there. The printout does not reflect your Social Security earnings by year, so if you suspect that your estimated benefit is inaccurate, you'll have to schedule an appointment with your local Social Security office to get year-by-year earnings. It's going to be up to you to find mistakes and get them corrected. This is less important for CSRS, because you don't have Social Security as part of your benefits for your federal employment years.

- A copy of your marriage license. The Office of Personnel Management actually requires you to send in a copy of your marriage certificate with your retirement paperwork. This is because some of your former colleagues were trying to give survivor benefits to people they weren't actually married to, so now you have to prove that you're married to the person you want to receive those benefits.

- If you are divorced, you're also going to want to keep a copy of the divorce decree in this important documents folder, even if your former spouse was not awarded any of your federal benefits. You want to just make sure that you have a copy of it there, so that you can prove that if it comes up.

- The last four documents you'll want to have in your folder are all beneficiary forms. The first one is what happens if you pass away before you actually get to retire; it designates who gets your last paycheck. You probably completed this form early in your career and might not have looked at it since that time. You may not like that person anymore, you may not even be married to that person anymore, so if you aren't sure who you named, now might be a good time to go back and redo the form (Form SF1152 is available at www.opm.gov).

- The second form, TSP-3, designates who inherits your TSP if you pass away (It is available at www.tsp.gov).

- The third form designates who gets your FEGLI – your group life insurance (Form SF1153 is available at www.opm.gov).

- And the final beneficiary form designates who gets your contributions to the retirement system (Form SF2808 is available at www.opm.gov). Every pay period, you're making a contribution to the Civil Service Retirement System. If you should pass away before you collect all of those contributions back through the benefits of your pension, that lump of money is inheritable, so you want to make sure you've named a beneficiary.

How Your Annuity Will Be Calculated

Now that we know you're eligible to retire, how are they going to calculate your annuity? Your annuity will be calculated on three things; your retirement service computation date, your "high three," and a formula that is based on your years of service.

Let's start with your retirement service computation date. When you look at your leave and earnings statement you'll see a date that says "SCD (service computation date) for leave purposes." This means that you may have had the right to accumulate leave at a faster rate based on when you started. Many people assume, "Oh, that's my SCD for retirement. That's the date that they're going use to calculate whether I have 30 years or not." Remember Carmen? Not necessarily so!

Your retirement service computation date is based on your federal service from the day you were appointed to the day you separated from service, whether you quit or you retired, as long as you were paying into the retirement system. The key point here is that you have to be paying into the system – making contributions. If you started work for the federal government and you were what was called a "co-op," or intern, or you were under temporary service, in all likelihood you were not paying into the retirement system.

While they gave you credit for that time towards accruing leave, it's not creditable for the calculation of your annuity, so we need to make some adjustments for those dates. Your retirement service computation date does include leave without pay up to six months in a calendar year. It includes part-time service, prior to April 7th of 1986. Even if you worked part-time for five years at half time, all five years count. After April 7th of 1986, part-time service counts towards eligibility, but when we calculate your annuity it's going be prorated. We'll talk about that in more detail in Chapter Three—"A Series of Unique Events."

The retirement service computation date also includes WAE – "when actually employed" time – where 260 days counts as a full year for these employees. The only other ways to adjust your service com- putation date for retirement purposes are by paying back a deposit for that temporary time when you didn't pay in; or paying a redeposit if you made contributions to the system, then left the federal government and took out those contributions, and subsequently returned to federal service. You can also add your military time in by paying a deposit. These are the only ways you have to adjust your service computation date.

Your "high three" is one of the federal benefits that has been under attack and review for a number of years. There are people in Washington who think that it should be changed to the "high five," because it would save the government money. It actually used to be the "high five" for CSRS employees, but in the early '70s it was changed to the "high three." While changing it to the "high five" would have something of a negative impact on your annuity, it's not earth shattering and probably won't amount to more than a thousand dollars a year.

Your "high three" is based on your highest three consecutive years of earnings in the federal government. It doesn't have to be three calendar years. It includes base plus locality pay. Nothing else – no cash awards, holiday pay, overtime pay, or military pay – is included in that "high three." It's your base plus locality pay. Once we know your highest three years of earnings and take the average, we know your high three number.

Now, what we really want to figure out is the formula that you're going to use to calculate your pension. What percentage of your "high three" are you going to use to calculate your estimated annuity?

Creditable Service Worksheet	Year	Month	Day
Planned Retirement Date			
Retirement Service Computation Date			
Creditable Service (Line 1 – Line 2)			
Unused Sick Leave (Use conversion chart)			
Total Creditable Service (Line 3 + Line 4)			

Using this worksheet, start by putting in when you plan to retire. Then, write in your retirement service computation date on the lines below your retirement date. Now, we're going do some math. Start on the right side and subtract the days. Then, subtract the months. Last, subtract the years. Now you have your years and months of creditable service.

Creditable Service Worksheet	Year	Month	Day
Planned Retirement Date	2013	1	3
Retirement Service Computation Date	1974	6	28
Creditable Service (Line 1 – Line 2)	38	6	5
Unused Sick Leave (Use conversion chart)			
Total Creditable Service (Line 3 + Line 4)			

In addition to this, you get to add sick leave. Any hours of unused sick leave that you have at the end of your career now turn into months, days, and maybe even years, depending on how much you have. Add that to your creditable service for calculation purposes of your annuity.

Creditable Service Worksheet	Year	Month	Day
Planned Retirement Date	2013	1	3
Retirement Service Computation Date	1974	6	28
Creditable Service (Line 1 – Line 2)	38	6	5
Unused Sick Leave (Use conversion chart)		6	26
Total Creditable Service (Line 3 + 4)	39	1	1

Sick Leave Chart

# of Days	0 Months +	1 Months +	2 Months +	3 Months +	4 Months +	5 Months +	6 Months +	7 Months +	8 Months +	9 Months +	10 Months +	11 Months +
0	0	174	348	522	696	870	1044	1217	1391	1565	1739	1913
1	6	180	354	528	701	875	1049	1223	1397	1571	1745	1919
2	12	186	359	533	707	881	1055	1229	1403	1577	1751	1925
3	17	191	365	539	713	887	1061	1235	1409	1583	1757	1930
4	23	197	371	545	719	893	1067	1241	1415	1588	1762	1936
5	29	203	377	551	725	899	1072	1246	1420	1594	1768	1942
6	35	209	383	557	730	904	1078	1252	1426	1600	1774	1948
7	41	214	388	562	736	910	1084	1258	1432	1606	1780	1954
8	46	220	394	568	742	916	1090	1264	1438	1612	1786	1959
9	52	226	400	574	748	922	1096	1270	1444	1617	1791	1965
10	58	232	406	580	754	928	1101	1275	1449	1623	1797	1971
11	64	238	412	586	759	933	1107	1281	1455	1629	1803	1977
12	70	243	417	591	765	939	1113	1287	1461	1635	1809	1983
13	75	249	423	597	771	945	1119	1293	1467	1641	1815	1988
14	81	255	429	603	777	951	1125	1299	1472	1646	1820	1994
15	87	261	435	609	783	957	1131	1304	1478	1652	1826	2000
16	93	267	441	615	788	962	1136	1310	1484	1658	1832	2006
17	99	272	446	620	794	968	1142	1316	1490	1664	1838	2012
18	104	278	452	626	800	974	1148	1322	1496	1670	1844	2017
19	110	284	458	632	806	980	1154	1328	1501	1675	1849	2023
20	116	290	464	638	812	986	1159	1333	1507	1681	1855	2029
21	122	296	470	643	817	991	1165	1339	1513	1687	1861	2035
22	128	301	475	649	823	997	1171	1345	1519	1693	1867	2041
23	133	307	481	655	829	1003	1177	1351	1525	1699	1873	2046
24	139	313	487	661	835	1009	1183	1357	1530	1704	1878	2052
25	145	319	493	667	841	1015	1189	1362	1536	1710	1884	2058
26	151	325	499	672	846	1020	1194	1368	1542	1716	1890	2064
27	157	330	504	678	852	1026	1200	1374	1548	1722	1896	2070
28	162	336	510	684	858	1032	1206	1380	1554	1728	1902	2075
29	168	342	516	690	864	1038	1212	1386	1559	1733	1907	2081

2,081 hours equals one year. If you have more sick leave than that, you subtract 2,081 from the number of hours you have, and you're going have one year, plus the number of months and days left over from that 2,081. In the example above, we used 1,194 hours of sick leave, which equated to 6 months and 26 days.

What's the most sick leave I've ever heard of anyone accumulating? Two gentlemen I know of, both strangely enough from the same town in southwestern Colorado, accumulated more than 6,000 hours of sick leave during their careers under CSRS.

If you're like most CSRS employees, you always saved your sick leave, and didn't use it if you didn't have to. Now you get to use it! Add your sick leave days to any days you had left over from that initial calculation, and if it equals 30 days, you get to add another month to your creditable service. If it doesn't add up to a month you get to contract something known as the "CSRS flu," which means that you're going try to use up those days before you retire. You want to calculate this very carefully.

Now we know how many years and how many months of service you're going to have your benefits calculated on. The easiest way to get your formula is to take those years and months, and turn them into a decimal. Let's say you have exactly 34 years of service. We're going to subtract two, then multiply it by 2, and we're going add .25%.

For that person with 34 years of service, when we subtract two we get 32. When we multiply that by two, we get 64, and then we add .25%. By these calculations, your annuity will be based on 64.25% of your "high three." If you had 34½ years, we'd do 34.5 minus 2, times 2, plus the .25%. That's the easiest way to get the formula that you're going to use to determine what your annual annuity is going to be.

Once we know what your annual annuity is going to be, we can divide that number by 12, which tells us what your gross monthly annuity will be. This is before taxes, before insurance and, if you're married, before we take out for survivor benefits. (Keep in mind if there's any change after we divide by 12, OPM "keeps the change.")

It's important for you to understand the moving parts of how OPM calculates your annuity, because you're going to get an estimate from your HR department before you retire. You may decide to work with a financial advisor, and he or she might give you an estimate as well. If HR sends you something different than what you've calculated, you want to be able to say, "Wait a minute. I recognize that this isn't right because I know how it should have been calculated." OPM is currently using the estimate provided by your agency when your retirement application is being processed to determine your "interim payment." This is the amount you receive while you're waiting for your retirement claim to be adjudicated. To be sure your interim payment is as high as possible, you want to understand these moving parts and exactly what goes into calculating a federal pension so your estimate is accurate.

For CSRS, we've covered how we're going to calculate your annuity, and what the best day to retire is. We've talked about your sick leave and managing that sick leave. Keep in mind; you want to make sure that you don't look at your sick leave in isolation. In other words, when you've calculated those hours and you see how many months and days you're going to have, you don't want to just look at that number and say, "Oh, I'm going to have 6 months and 26 days, so I'm going to use my 26 days of sick leave up and just count the 6 months toward my annuity," because we know that if you had at least 4 days left over from your creditable service, it would count as another month when added to that 26 days. That's why we don't want you to look at those sick leave hours by themselves. You want to add them to your actual creditable service before you determine just exactly how long you're going to be "in quarantine" before retirement.

Military Service and CSRS

Under the CSRS system, if you are retired military and you're receiving military pay, it makes no sense for you to stop taking that wonderful military benefit in order to buy back that time to have it count under CSRS. You're going to want to keep receiving that military retirement pay.

If you have military service and you entered federal service before October 1, 1982, you are allowed to count your military time toward your CSRS service for retirement purposes without paying a deposit for that service. However, if you are eligible for Social Security at age 62, your CSRS annuity will be recalculated without that military service, and you will receive a lower CSRS annuity at that time. This provision is known as "Catch-62."

The key here is to understand whether you are eligible for Social Security at age 62 or are likely to become eligible by 62. Then you can make the determination of whether to pay back your military time. The majority of CSRS employees won't be eligible for Social Security at age 62, and they have nothing to worry about. They don't have to make the deposit, and they do get to count their military time.

If you have military service and you entered federal service after October 1, 1982, you're going to pay 7% of what your military pay was at the time. Were you highly compensated if you were in the military sometime in the late '70s or early '80s? Probably not, so 7% of that number isn't going to amount to a lot of money. However, the interest that they're going charge you on it is going to be worse than the cost of making the deposit itself. That said, it most likely will still make sense for you to make that deposit, because if you pay that time back you're going to get to count it all.

You're going to get to count that time towards the calculation of your annuity, and you're going to be paid that benefit for the rest of your life. If you have not paid it back yet and you're trying to determine whether or not it makes sense to pay back this military deposit, have your HR department or your financial advisor run your estimates both ways, and see what the monthly difference is between the two, then divide that into what the cost would be to make your military deposit. That's going to give you the number of months it would take you to recover that amount. If it's less than 10 years, and you think you're going to live longer than 10 years, it probably makes sense to go ahead and pay it back. If it looks like it would take you longer than 10 years to recoup it, then you may have to think long and hard about whether you actually want to make that payment or not.

How to Provide for Your Survivors

The best benefit that you get for having been a federal employee all these years is your pension. You get that pension for life, a benefit that has all but disappeared in the private sector, where even career employees are cut loose after 30-year careers with nothing but a handshake.

The second-best benefit that you get is receiving your health benefits for the rest of your life, with the federal government picking up 72% of your premium. The 28% you are responsible for is the same percentage you pay today. If you elect a survivor benefit for your spouse, you not only get to keep those health benefits for life, but so does your spouse.

You get access to the same health benefits you've had, and you get to access open season each year, which we'll talk about in Chapter Five – "Federal Employee Health Benefits." You can change your plan each and every year, and additionally you get some very special choices and options with Medicare that no other group receives. If you don't remember anything else from this chapter, and you're married, the one thing you want to take away is the importance of electing a survivor benefit for your spouse to allow you both to hang onto health benefits with the federal government continuing to pay a significant portion of the premium. Even if you, as the federal employee, choose to leave your spouse as little as one dollar of survivor benefits, your spouse still gets to keep your health benefits in the event of your passing away first.

Of course, most federal employees don't leave their spouses with just a dollar. You can leave them a maximum benefit, which is 55%. In order to leave your spouse 55%, it's going to cost you roughly 10% of your annuity. (The actual formula is 2.5% of the first $3,600 of your annual computed annuity plus 10% of any amount over that $3,600). You can opt to leave them anything between one dollar and the 55%. If you decide, "My spouse doesn't really need the financial support of the survivor benefit, but they really do need the health insurance," you could calculate the survivor benefit so it leaves your surviving spouse enough benefits to pay the health insurance premium. You'll want to consider the highest premium in OPM for a single person and leave your spouse something roughly 50% higher to pay those premiums, because the cost of healthcare is rising faster than the cost of living adjustments you get on your pension.

For example, if your share of the current highest premium for health benefits in your state (if that's where you plan to retire) is $200, you would add 50% to that amount. You would want to provide $300 a month, or $3,600 a year, to your surviving spouse. The actual calculation on your retirement paperwork is confusing on this topic, because it asks you to calculate 55% of the number you want to leave your survivor. Huh? The easiest way to get this number is to divide the annual amount you want to leave for your survivor by 55%. This will provide the number you'll write on your retirement paperwork. The $3,600 is an inexpensive amount because remember, the first $3,600 in survivor benefits only costs you 2.5% of your annuity. Everything above that would cost 10% of your annuity.

You can leave survivor benefits to your current spouse. Much to your current spouse's surprise, you may also leave it to a former spouse if a court orders it. You can leave it to an insurable interest, which is someone who is closer to you than a first cousin and who is financially dependent upon you. This may be someone like your parents who are now financially dependent upon you. It is not your 32-year-old child who simply doesn't want to work for a living (but believes he's financially dependent on you). Minor children are also covered up to the age of 18, and you don't pay anything extra for that. It's very generous of OPM to give you that benefit, but keep in mind that your minor children aren't going to be minors forever.

Another strategy married CSRS employees use to cover the survivorship benefit is to utilize life insurance instead of the survivor benefit. We know that the cost of the survivor benefit goes up each year, every time the retiree gets a cost of living adjustment on their pension. You might pay into that survivor benefit for 20 or 25 years. At that point, you might have paid in $100,000 or $150,000, but what happens if your spouse passes away first? That's right – OPM wins. They keep that lump sum. You no longer have to pay into that survivor benefit, but you do have to give up all the money that you've paid in up to that point.

Many people decide, "I'm going leave my spouse just enough of a survivor benefit to cover the health insurance premiums, and I'm going to take the difference of what I would have spent in the annuity and get some life insurance on myself. That way if my spouse passes away first, I can name another beneficiary."

Year	Age	Monthly Annuity w/out Survivor (A)	Monthly Annuity with Survivor (B)	Survivor Benefit Cost (A-B)	Survivor's Monthly Benefit (55% of A)	Annual Difference	Accum. Annual Diff.
1	55	3,928	3,559	370	2,161	4,440	4,440
20	75	6,862	6,240	649	3,789	7,794	119,427

This example illustrates how both the survivor benefit and the cost of the survivor benefit increase as the retiree receives COLA's each year. In 20 years, the total cost would be nearly $120,000!

Year	Age	Monthly Annuity w/out Survivor (A)	Monthly Annuity with Survivor (B)	Survivor Benefit Cost (A-B)	Survivor's Monthly Benefit (55% of A)	Annual Difference	Accum. Annual Diff.
1	55	3,928	3,903	25	259	300	300
20	75	6,862	6,821	41	425	492	8,044

By reducing the amount of the survivor benefit, the cost is reduced as well. The difference can then be used to purchase permanent life insurance coverage. Keep in mind that this strategy does not work in all cases, and it is important to analyze all factors, including the federal employee's health (ability to get life insurance coverage), age, amount of life insurance coverage available, your spouse's age, and ability of the surviving spouse to manage the life insurance proceeds.

How does Social Security affect the CSRS annuity?

Let's start by talking about those of you who fall into the category of CSRS Offset, which is that unique scenario in which you worked for the federal government, put in at least 5 years of service, then left the federal government prior to 1984, and subsequently returned to work for the government after at least a 1-year break in service.

If you returned to work *after* January 1st of 1984, Congress had determined that anyone hired in the federal government after January 1, 1984 was required to pay into Social Security. If you came back after that date and wanted to be in the Civil Service Retirement System, you were required to pay into Social Security. Consequently, you became part of a hybrid system known as the CSRS Offset, and you paid into both the CSRS system and Social Security.

If you are eligible for a pension based on employment that did not require you to pay into Social Security (i.e., CSRS), but you're still eligible for Social Security benefits, Social Security says, "Wait a minute." It's going look like you are a low-wage earner and you're going to get a higher benefit than you're really entitled to.

Social Security will apply something known as the Windfall Elimination Provision (WEP), which means that if you are eligible for Social Security *and* a CSRS pension, they are going to subtract something from your Social Security benefit. The amount that will be subtracted is based on how many years of substantial earnings you have under the Social Security system. If you want to know which years will count as substantial earnings years, you can get out your Social Security statement, then go to the SSA website page: www.ssa.gov/pubs/10045.html#amount.

Look at page three of your Social Security statement, where it lists all of your earnings over your lifetime, compare that with the years/earnings list you'll find on the Social Security website, and check off those years in which your earnings count as substantial earnings. If you can get to 30 years of substantial earnings during which you were paying into Social Security, you're not subject to the Windfall Elimination Provision. However, most CSRS employees can't meet that benchmark, because they paid into Social Security for fewer than 30 years. They might have paid in when they were in college, or maybe they worked a part-time job. If you have anything less than 30 years, your Social Security benefit will be reduced by an amount that is based on that number of years. If you have less than 20 years of substantial earnings, the maximum reduction taken for the WEP in 2011 is $381. If you have more than 20, but not 30, the deduction will come down year by year, based on that $381. But the maximum amount your Social Security can be reduced by is $381.

Now you may be thinking, "I'm not going to collect much, if anything, on my own Social Security benefit. But if my spouse is eligible for Social Security, while they're still alive I can collect half of their benefit. I think I'll just do that; I'll collect my nice CSRS pension, half my spouse's Social Security, and life should be pretty good in retirement."

Well, Congress is onto you again, and in 1986 they passed a provision known as the Government Pension Offset. If you have a government pension where you did not pay into Social Security, you may be eligible for a portion of your spouse's benefit. Here's how that amount will be determined.

Start with the benefit that you're eligible for from your spouse – half of your spouse's benefit – and subtract two-thirds of your pension. If there's anything left, you can have it. The only good news is that if it's a negative number they don't ask you to pay them!

The Voluntary Contribution Program

The Voluntary Contribution Program (VCP) is the best benefit for CSRS and CSRS Offset that most remaining employees have never heard of. It is something of a relic; it was created as a result of federal employees going to OPM and saying, "We contribute 7% of every paycheck to our retirement system, but we'd like the opportunity to be able to contribute even more than that, so that at the end of our careers, it would increase the amount of our annuity." A very popular way to do this at the time was a structure created for both municipal and state governments, which the federal government decided to utilize – the Voluntary Contribution Program.

The program was designed to put after-tax dollars into a fund that would earn a declared rate of return each year. This is a fixed interest rate declared annually by the Treasury Department. The funds grew tax-deferred, and when you retired, it tacked an additional benefit onto your pension. In 1987, the Thrift Savings Plan was created and at that point, the Voluntary Contribution Program went to the federal government's deepest, darkest storeroom. It wasn't thought about again for almost 20 years, because if you had access to the TSP where you could control how the funds were invested, you had more opportunity, so it made more sense to use the TSP.

In 2006, Congress passed the Pension Protection Act of 2006 and a congressman with a horse in the race at the very last moment added an earmark that said, "If you have a Voluntary Contribution Program, when you roll those funds out you can put them in a Roth IRA." Well, all of a sudden they had our attention! It was like, "Wow! You mean to tell me that I can make these contributions with after-tax dollars and earn interest on them, and then get a large chunk of money in a Roth IRA at the end of my career? That is a great deal."

CSRS and CSRS Offsets are eligible to contribute 10% of everything they ever made as a federal employee, so the amounts that can be contributed often range anywhere from $125,000 to $250,000. When you consider that the amount you can contribute to a traditional Roth IRA each year is $5,000, or $6,000 if you happen to be age 50 or older, this is a huge windfall for CSRS employees. It provides the opportunity to get significant amounts of assets into a Roth IRA right at the end of their careers.

Some rules you'll need to know include: You cannot owe a deposit or a re-deposit. If you owe those, you have to pay them back before you can contribute. And you cannot have participated in the program in the past and taken your funds out. You're going to apply for a VCP account number using SF-2804. It is the shortest government form you're ever going to fill out, and the easiest. You answer three simple questions — do you owe a deposit? Do you owe a re-deposit? Have you ever participated in the VCP before? Then you're going to have HR sign off on the form, and you send it off to

OPM (the address is included on the form). In 10 to 14 days, you'll get back a VCP account number, and you're ready to start making contributions.

You can put in as little or as much as you want, up to your maximum level. It has to be contributed in $25 increments, so you can't send them $472.16. It has to be divisible by $25. You can send in as many deposits as you want. Once you have it fully funded, even if you're still working, you can transfer those funds right back out to a Roth IRA. Any interest that you earn will be taxable. You'll pay the taxes on those earnings, and then the entire amount will be a Roth IRA and will grow tax-free for the remainder of your life.

CHAPTER TWO

FERS—My Plan's Better Than Your Plan

I f you're under the FERS system, you've heard your entire career how much better someone else's retirement plan is compared to yours. It's true that a FERS pension is smaller than a CSRS pension with the same circumstances, and that more of the responsibility is placed on the FERS employee to contribute, through the Thrift Savings Plan, to their own retirement. The other side of that is the FERS employee has more control of his pension investments, and thus greater opportunity to provide for his own wellbeing. Thousands of FERS employees, such as Karen, who you'll meet below, retire successfully each year.

Upon exiting the elevator on the 5th floor of the VA hospital, a sign with a big red arrow greeted me, "If you're here about the money – head this way." At the next hallway, "10 steps to the second left," encouraged me to forge ahead. The signs continued to get funnier as they guided me through the maze of the cardiac ward until I came to an office that said, "You've arrived! Come on in and bring me good news."

To the untrained visitor without a GPS, a VA hospital can seem like a maze, but Karen made the journey fun. As a cardiac nurse, most of her patients were extremely nervous when they came under her care. She recognized that anything she could do to ease that tension made the patient experience better. Karen used the same conscientiousness to make sure that I got to her office where she was anxiously awaiting the results of her "tests" – otherwise known as her retirement analysis.

Over and over I am dazzled by the dedication of the federal worker, whether at the Department of Energy or the Department of Education, Health and Human Services or Homeland Security, USDA or WAPA or VA. Over 2 million FERS employees go to work every day, getting the job done and hopefully, enjoying a little sense of adventure along the way. You may not hear it much these days – thank you for all you do.

The FERS Retirement System was created early in the 1980s for federal employees, which was the largest group of employees in our country at the time. Prior to the creation of FERS, federal employees didn't pay into Social Security. Congress looked around and said, "Okay, we think Social Security might be in trouble. You know what we should do? We should get those federal employees to pay into Social Security." Thus, the new Federal Employee Retirement System was born.

Anyone hired after January 1, 1984, who did not have at least 5 years of service by January 1, 1987, is required to pay into Social Security, and the Federal Employee Retirement System. Those who were hired after January 1 of 1987 normally contribute 7% of their pay to their retirement; 6.2% goes to Social Security, and 0.8% to FERS. We have seen in the past year where they've actually reduced the Social Security contribution to 4.2%, but you're still going to contribute 0.8% to the FERS Retirement System.

A hybrid of the FERS system includes those people who were in CSRS at one time and opted to go into FERS of their own accord. We know that anyone who was hired after January 1, 1984, who didn't have at least 5 years of federal employment on January 1, 1987, automatically had to go into FERS. However, employees who had at least five years of CSRS employment were offered the opportunity to go to this new retirement system three times; in 1987, 1988, and 1998. That's one way you could become a FERS Transferee. A Transferee's annuity is calculated as if he was a CSRS employee for his CSRS years, then all the years after he became a FERS Transferee are calculated under FERS.

The other way to become a FERS Transferee is to have worked for the federal government and had at least 5 years of service under CSRS or as a CSRS Offset, and leave federal service. If you came back after one year or more, you could choose to go into the FERS system. One of the benefits offered to get you to come into FERS was portability. If you thought you weren't going to stay with the federal government, then FERS was more portable. A third of a FERS retiree's income in retirement is designed to come from the Thrift Savings Plan, and that Thrift Savings Plan is portable, where the larger annuity that the CSRS offers is not portable. You can't take it with you to another job; you have to wait until you're old enough to actually receive the benefit.

How and When Do I Qualify for My Annuity?

In order to retire on an immediate, unreduced annuity, a FERS employee has to meet certain criteria: You have to reach a certain age, and you have to have a certain number of years of service in order to qualify.

If you were born	Your FERS MRA is:
before 1948	55
in 1948	55 and 2 months
in 1949	55 and 4 months
in 1950	55 and 6 months
in 1951	55 and 8 months
in 1952	55 and 10 months
in 1953 – 1964	56
in 1965	56 and 2 months
in 1966	56 and 4 months
in 1967	56 and 6 months
in 1968	56 and 8 months
in 1969	56 and 10 months
1970 or after	57

You must have reached your MRA and have 30 years of service; or you can be 60 years old and have 20 years of service; or you can be 62 years old with only 5 years of service and be eligible to retire on an immediate, unreduced annuity. We're seeing more and more people come to the federal government at the end of their careers in order to work the last 5 to 10 years within the federal government. The biggest benefit of doing this is that they get to take their health care benefits with them into retirement.

Under FERS, you have the option to take a voluntary early-out. This means that if you attain your MRA and you have as little as 10 years of service, you can retire on an immediate annuity; however, your benefit is reduced by 5/12 of 1% for each month that you're under age 62. An easier way to think of this is that it's 5% a year. For example, let's say that you reach your MRA of 57, you have at least 10 years of service, and you want to retire. You don't want to wait until you're 60; you don't want to wait until you're 62. You can retire on an immediate annuity; however, there's going to be a penalty attached to your annuity and deducted from it of 5% for every year that you're under age 62. A 57-year-old would be 5 years under age 62; he would take a 25% penalty against his annuity, and that penalty is permanent. It doesn't end when he turns 62. But it is a way for people who want to leave the federal government early and take an immediate annuity to do that.

One exception to this is if you are retiring on your MRA with 10 years of service and you say, "I don't really want to pay that penalty, and I could live without my annuity for a few years. I plan to go get another job somewhere else anyway." You could actually defer taking your annuity until you are age 60, if you have at least 20 years of service, or age 62 if you have less than 20 years of service when you leave. You can pick up your annuity at that point without the penalty.

You might also be offered an involuntary early-out that would allow you to take an immediate annuity without any reduction. You're eligible to take this "early-out" offer at age 50 with 20 years of service, or any age with 25 years of service. These offers are called VERAs, which is where your agency goes to OPM and petitions for Voluntary Early Reduction Authority. The agency has to get OPM's approval to reduce its workforce. Next, the agency determines which jobs and functions it could do without, and then they make that offer to you. If you are 50 years old with 20 years of service or any age with 25 years of service, you're allowed to retire on an immediate annuity and avoid the reduction.

Depending on the composition of the agency workforce, offering a VERA may not get the number of volunteers for the early-out they want. It may become necessary for the agency to go back to OPM and ask for permission to offer a Voluntary Separation Incentive Payment or VSIP to their employees to "sweeten the pot." You'll also hear these payments referred to as buyouts, and they usually amount to $25,000. Some agencies offer less, but at this time it cannot be more than $25,000.

What Are the Best Dates to Retire?

That's a question we hear quite commonly. Of course, the best date to retire is when you become eligible and you decide you're ready. But in addition to that, we can line up certain things to make sure that you maximize the value of your benefits.

For a FERS employee, retiring on the last day of the month allows you to make the most of your benefits, because you're paid through that last day of the month and your annuity begins on the first day of the following month, so you don't have any days that are unpaid. If you can combine that last day of the month with the end of a pay period, you will accrue four hours of sick leave and eight hours of annual leave for that pay period. In the grand scheme of things, this is not going to make or break your retirement, but if you can make sure that all those pieces line up, it's just one more little added benefit.

Most federal employees, about 70%, retire on the last day of the year, because they are allowed to roll over their maximum annual leave at that point. Each year, you can carry over 240 hours of annual leave. If you do not take any leave during your final year of employment, you will accrue another 208 hours, so if you retire on the last day of the year, you are going to be paid out for 448 hours of annual leave at your hourly rate, you're going to receive a cost of living adjustment on that leave if there's a cost of living that year, and you get to pay your taxes in the new year. That lump sum doesn't go on top of a full year's salary; it gets combined with your pension in the following year and could cause you to have a lower effective tax rate.

The best dates to retire in 2012 are:

FERS

- January 31
- February 29
- March 31
- April 30
- May 31 (holiday!)
- June 30 (also end of pay period)
- July 31
- August 31
- September 30
- October 31
- November 30
- December 31

If you're not quite ready to retire in 2012, you can get a list of the best dates to retire over the next 10 years here.

www.annvanderslice.com/best-dates-to-retire/

Calculating Your Annuity

Once you become eligible and you've determined the best date, now you want to calculate your federal annuity. It's based on three things: your years of service based on your retirement service computation date, your "high three" salary, and a formula.

Your retirement service computation date is based on the time between when you were hired and when you separate, as long as retirement deductions were being withheld. As long as that 0.8% that goes into FERS is being withheld, the time counts. It includes up to six months of leave without pay in a calendar year; it includes all part-time service prior to April 7, 1986. If you have part-time service on or after April 7, 1986, it includes credit for the eligibility in order to qualify to calculate your annuity, but when the annuity is actually calculated, that time is going to be prorated. For example, if you worked 5 years at 50% time, it's going to be prorated, and the amount used to calculate your annuity would only be 2½ years; 50% of 5 years would be 2½. Intermittent days worked also count toward your service computation date. As we'll talk about in Chapter

Three—"A Series of Unique Events," the only other ways to add to your service time are by paying back for military service, making a deposit for service where your retirement contributions were not withheld, or making a redeposit.

Annual leave for FERS employees is based on how many years of service you have.

Employee Type	Less than 3 years of service	3 years but less than 15 years of service	15 or more years of service
Full-time employees	½ day (4 hours) for each pay period	3/4 day (6 hours) for each pay period, except 1 ¼ day (10 hours) in last pay period	1 day (8 hours) for each pay period
Part-time employees	1 hour of annual leave for each 20 hours in a pay status	1 hour of annual leave for each 13 hours in a pay status	1 hour of annual leave for each 10 hours in a pay status

Full-time employees with less than 3 years of service earn 4 hours, or a half a day, of leave for each pay period. If you have 3 years of service but less than 15, that bumps up to ¾ of a day, or 6 hours, for each pay period, except you get a day and a quarter for the last pay period. And finally, once you have 15 years of federal service, you are going to get 8 hours of accrued annual leave for each and every pay period, or 208 hours per year. Part-time employees with less than 3 years of service accrue 1 hour of annual leave for each 20 hours in pay status. When they reach that 3-year anniversary, they receive 1 hour of annual leave for every 13 hours in pay status, and finally, once they have over 15 years of service, they receive 1 hour of annual leave for every 10 hours in pay status. They are allowed to carry over 240 hours of annual leave each year. If you have any more than 240 hours, it's known as "use or lose." At the end your career, you're paid for unused annual leave.

Sick leave is not based on your years of service; you simply accrue 4 hours of sick leave for every pay period. Prior to January 1, 2014, FERS employees who are ready to retire will be allowed to add 50% of their sick leave to their creditable service for the calculation of their annuity. After January 1, 2014, FERS retirees will be allowed to count all of their sick leave. If you're considering retiring in the middle of 2013 versus the end of the year, depending on how much sick leave you have, this might be a determining factor.

Your high three salary is the next component that we need to know in order to calculate your FERS annuity. The high three average is the average of your base plus locality pay, over any three consecutive years of creditable service. It does not include anything other than base plus locality pay; no bonuses, holiday pay, overtime pay, military pay, travel pay or cash awards count toward your high three average. It's simply your base plus locality pay over any three consecutive years. Typically, it is your last three years of service, but it doesn't have to be.

And finally, we're going to apply a formula to that high three average in order to come up with your annual annuity. You receive 1% for each year of service, multiplied by your high three. If you work for 30 years, you're going to get 30% of your high three. If you work for 25 years, you're going to get 25% of your high three. If you work until you are 62 and you have at least 20 years of service, you'll receive a 10% bonus on your annuity. You get to use 1.1% times each of those years of service, instead of 1%. Using the numbers from the previous example, if you were 62 years old when you retired with 30 years of service, you would get 33% of your high three as opposed to 30%, which is a 10% boost.

Survivor Benefits

There are two survivor benefits available to FERS retirees. If you are married, you can provide your spouse with either a 25% benefit or a 50% benefit. The cost for the 25% benefit is 5% of your annuity, and for the 50% benefit, it's 10% of your annuity. This survivor benefit is available to your current spouse; much to your current spouse's surprise, it is also available to a former spouse if it was indicated in the divorce decree or by court order. It is available to an insurable interest, which is someone who is closer to you than a first cousin who is financially dependent upon you (for instance, a special needs child); and it is available to your minor children.

A key point on survivor benefits is that the retiree must elect at least a minimum survivor benefit for his spouse, in order for the spouse to continue receiving health benefits if the employee passes away first. One of the great benefits that you have in addition to your pension is the fact that you get to continue your health benefits into retirement for both you and your spouse as long as you're both alive, with the federal government paying 72% of the premium and you paying 28%. This occurs as long as you make sure to keep that survivor benefit for your spouse. You make this election at retirement when you complete your retirement paperwork.

One thing that concerns federal employees is the feeling that they might not even make it to retirement. What happens if you die at your desk? (Sometimes it feels like that, doesn't it?)

With at least 18 months of creditable service but prior to retirement, your survivor would receive a lump sum benefit of $29,722, which is adjusted annually for inflation, plus half of the greater of your high three average or your current salary. Additionally, with at least 10 years of creditable service, your surviving spouse would receive not only the lump sum benefit from above, but also 50% of your annuity calculated as of the date of your death. It would be presumed that you would have elected the 50% survivor benefit for your spouse, and they would automatically get 50% of your annuity. If they were on your health insurance, they would automatically continue with those health benefits as well. Any Social Security or other survivor benefits are not affected by these lump sum payments.

Disability

There are many great benefits for FERS, but one thing missing from the plan is either short-term or long-term disability insurance. Sick leave acts as a short-term disability policy; the only alternative for long-term disability is a disability retirement. It's available if you are no longer able to do your job in your current position, and you are not qualified for any other position in the same location at the same grade and pay.

Disability retirement doesn't mean that you can't work; you are allowed to get another job and still receive a disability retirement. If you are eligible for a disability retirement, you may make up to 80% of your federal pay in a private sector job. You will continue your health and life insurance coverage as long as you were previously insured for the 5 years before you apply for the disability retirement.

You have to have worked for the federal government for at least 18 months, and you have to apply for benefits. If you are incapacitated and not capable of applying for yourself, then your agency, a guardian, or another interested person can apply for you. You must also apply for Social Security disability benefits. It does not mean that you must be awarded Social Security disability benefits, but you must at least apply. And if you meet those requirements, and are approved, your benefits will be calculated as follows.

The first year, you will get 60% of your high three, less any benefits you may be awarded from Social Security. These benefits are taxable. After that first year and beyond, you're going to get 40% of your high three, less 60% of any benefits that you receive from Social Security.

Social Security disability benefits are fairly hard to qualify for; the requirements are stringent, so it's likely that in that first year, you may not be receiving Social Security benefits. You may have to wait until the end of that second or third year for Social Security disability to finally kick in. At age 62, your disability benefit will be recalculated as if you had worked all those years up to age 62, and then it will be calculated just as a regular FERS annuity would be calculated. Of course, your high three from when you first qualified for the disability retirement will be used in that recalculation.

Social Security and the FERS Retiree

The FERS system has three components: the FERS annuity, which we've just talked about, Social Security, and the Thrift Savings Plan. The earliest age that Social Security is available is age 62, but when we looked at the eligibility to retire, we saw that many FERS employees have an MRA (Minimum Retirement Age) of 55, 56, and no higher than 57. Yet at that point you wouldn't be eligible for Social Security, so OPM came up with what's known as the FERS supplement.

If you retire at your MRA and have 30 years of service, or you retire at age 60 with 20 years of service, you are eligible for this payment, which comes directly from OPM into your bank account to supplement your pension until you are eligible for Social Security. If you choose not to take Social Security at age 62, OPM doesn't keep paying you. They stop your benefits at age 62, whether or not you take Social Security. Your FERS supplement is calculated based on your years of FERS service divided by 40. This is actual FERS service – so if you've purchased military time, it's going be subtracted before dividing by 40. That's going to give you a fraction that will be multiplied times the Social Security benefit that is projected for you at age 62. You can find this estimate by going to www.ssa.gov/estimator and putting in your information. It will pull up your Social Security record and tell you what your age 62 benefit will be. If you have 30 years of creditable service you would divide 30 by 40, which would give you 30/40, or 75% of that Social Security benefit.

While you are earning this FERS supplement, it has the same earnings limitations as when you take Social Security at age 62. This means that if you think you're going to go out and get the "fun" job when you retire, as well as collect your pension and collect your Social Security supplement and take money from your TSP – well, that fun job better not pay very well, because your FERS supplement is subject to the Social Security earnings test, which for 2012 is $14,640. If you earn more than $14,640, for every $2 over that that you earn, you will give $1 back out of your Social Security or your FERS supplement. Social Security benefits are covered extensively in the Social Security chapter.

Every few years, a rumor spreads through federal agencies that FERS retirees aren't entitled to full Social Security benefits and that they are subject to something called the Windfall Elimination Provision (WEP). Unless you are a FERS Transferee, you will not be covered under the WEP.

You do not have to worry about not being able to collect your Social Security benefits. The FERS retiree receives three components: his pension, Social Security, and the TSP. The WEP does NOT apply to retirees who earn a pension where they paid into Social Security, which FERS retirees did.

COLA's

In retirement, you will receive cost of living adjustments based on a percentage of the Consumer Price Index for Urban and Clerical Wage Earners (CPI-W). If the CPI-W measured as of September 30 is between 0% and 2%, the FERS retiree gets all of that increase awarded on December 1 and it shows up on their January 1 annuity payment. If the CPI-W is between 2% and 3%, FERS retirees get a flat 2%, and a CPI-W anywhere over 3% provides the CPI minus 1% as their cost of living increase.

The first year after retirement, if you retire in the middle of the year, your Cost of Living Adjustment (COLA) will be prorated. The most important thing for the FERS retiree to remember is that you will NOT receive your first COLA until you reach age 62. This can be an important thing to consider if you are retiring at your MRA of 56 years old, and we have a burst of inflation in our economy of, say, 3% a year. Between 56 and 62, you would have 6 years, or 18%, that your pension would have fallen behind the actual economy until you get your first COLA. It is even more important when you consider that many people going into retirement in the near future may not have gotten any cost of living increases during their final working years. Your salary may have been frozen for a few years, and that combined with the lack of a retirement COLA until age 62 can have a big negative effect on your overall retirement income.

CHAPTER THREE

A Series of Unique Events

Part-time, Deposits and Offsets – Oh my!

A s Chris laid out her paperwork on the desk, it seemed like one of those magic tricks where the hankies just keep coming out of a small object. With seven different periods of part-time service at three different agencies (all at different hours per pay period), a break in service (where she'd withdrawn her retirement contributions), and military service (for which she had not made a deposit), no one had ever been able to provide a reasonable estimate of her retirement benefits.

Even seasoned benefits officers can be challenged when one employee has such a complicated record. It was important for Chris to understand the components involved in calculating each of her "unique events." All of these events are allowed for federal workers – it's how they affect your overall retirement that can be overwhelming.

After some education on part-time service and its effect on retirement, what it means to be a CSRS Offset (and why you always hear it's the best of all systems), and developing a plan for repaying her military deposit, Chris left feeling in control of her federal service. Knowledge is power!

Covered in this chapter will be all those things that can put a little twist on the calculation of your benefits. We'll talk about deposits and redeposits, part-time service and buying back military time, and how these unique events might affect the calculation of your annuity.

The definition of a deposit is when an employee has had a period or periods of service where he or she did not contribute into his or her retirement, either CSRS or FERS. This may include seasonal time or co-op time; you may have been an intern. You came to work for the government, you were paid by the government, but you weren't a full-time or a career-conditional employee, and so they weren't withholding retirement deductions because it wasn't clear whether you were going to stay with the government.

If you later became a full-time employee, you may want to count that time towards the calculation of your annuity and certainly towards being eligible. Under the CSRS system, if you have service prior to October 1, 1982, and you have not made a deposit for that time, 100% of it counts towards the eligibility. However, your annuity will be reduced by 10% of the deposit owed that you should have paid back. Keep in mind that it's not just the amount of the deposit, but the accrued interest together with the amount of that deposit, that you'll need to consider when determining whether to pay it. The longer you wait to pay it back, the larger that sum becomes.

Deposits almost always occur from time worked at the beginning of your career, and sometimes you don't think about paying it back until near the end of your career when interest has accrued and can make a pretty large difference in the amount that you owe. If you make the deposit, of course, you get to count it for eligibility and the annuity computation in all cases. For service prior to October 1, 1982, you make the deposit; it all counts. If you have service after October 1, 1982, if you do not make the deposit, you get to count the time for being eligible but get no credit for your annuity computation. It doesn't go into that calculation at all; it gets deducted from it. That can have a significant impact on your annuity.

In the FERS system, if you have service prior to January 1, 1989, and make the deposit, you're going to get to count it. If you do not make the deposit, you get no credit for eligibility or the annuity computation. That's a significant point for FERS employees who have any non-creditable, non-deposit service prior to January 1, 1989. In most cases, they're going to want to make that deposit because they're going to want to get to count the time both for eligibility and the calculation of their annuity. For FERS, if a deposit is owed for any service after January 1, 1989, you aren't even given the option to make a deposit. It's not allowed.

What are the pros and cons? Should you make that deposit? Under CSRS, for that initial deposit for the service prior to October 1, 1982, a general rule of thumb is that it often makes sense to make the deposit. If your deposit isn't made, your annuity is reduced by 10% of the amount due, and conventional wisdom would dictate that if you think you're going live longer than 10 years in retirement, you'd repay the deposit, because even though it's reduced by 10%, and presumably in 10 years your deposit would be repaid, they continue to take that deduction long after the 10 years are up. So if you think you're going to live longer than 10 years and you want to bet on yourself, you may want to repay that deposit plus interest.

For a CSRS employee, if the deposit for service after October 1, 1982, isn't made, you don't get any credit for the annuity computation. You're going to want to have the calculation run on your pension both with and without the deposit. Divide the difference between those two options into how much you owe to determine how many months it would take to recover the deposit. Again, if it will take you less than 10 years to recover it, you might want to consider repaying it. In most instances, the redeposit amount (original amount plus interest) will be so high that you won't want to repay it, but there are cases where you will, so you want to run the numbers to be sure.

Under FERS for the service prior to January 1, 1989, you're going to do the same thing we just described for CSRS. You're going to run the annuity calculation, both with and without the deposit, take the difference between the two, and divide it into the overall deposit amount plus interest that's owed to get the number of months it would take to recover that deposit. Then make the determination whether you think you're going to live longer than that, and act accordingly.

On redeposits, this applies to an employee who worked for the federal government and paid into the retirement system, then left federal service. When employees leave federal service, they all say the same thing: "I'm never coming back." And they take a refund of their contributions – that 0.8% that they contribute to FERS or the

7% that they contribute to CSRS – and they say, "That was all my money. I put it in the system. I would like it all back, please."

Well, many of them then did what they said they were never going do: They came back to work for the government. They found out that the grass wasn't necessarily greener on the private sector side of the street. If they want their prior time to count, they have to repay what they took out – make a redeposit – in order for it to count for their eligibility and the calculation of their annuity.

In all cases, if you left federal service and you did not take your contributions out and they were not refunded, you don't have anything to worry about. They're still sitting there with your name on them, just waiting for you to come back to work for the federal government. You don't need to do anything.

But if your contributions were refunded for CSRS contributions, if your service ended before October 1, 1990, and you do not make your redeposit, you get to count all the time for the eligibility, but your annuity will be actuarially reduced. What that means is the guys with the little green eyeshades (they're known as actuaries) will sit around and try to calculate how long they think you're going to live, and based on that number of years, they're going to reduce your annuity accordingly, and hopefully, they will have recovered all of that money by the time you reach your life expectancy. (Not all people comply with the actuaries, by the way!)

If your service ended after September 30, 1990, and you do not make that redeposit, you still get to count it for your eligibility, but it doesn't count at all in the calculation of your annuity. So your benefit isn't reduced; it simply doesn't count at all.

Under FERS, if your contributions were refunded and you do not make the redeposit, it does not count for either eligibility purposes or annuity purposes, so in most cases it will make sense to make that redeposit under FERS. This redeposit previously was not allowed; it was only legislation that passed in 2009, which allowed FERS employees to begin counting their sick leave in the calculation of their pension, that provided that FERS employees could make a redeposit of funds they previously had withdrawn.

Should you make that redeposit? For CSRS, if the service was prior to October 1, 1990, we know that over 20 years of interest gets added to the original amount that was refunded. The interest is typically more than the original refund, sometimes much more; often more than the employee can afford to put back into that redeposit. It often makes sense not to pay it back and take the reduction to your pension.

For FERS, because that contribution level is smaller, what you would have withdrawn was a lower amount and the timeframe is shorter. It may still make sense to make that redeposit. You're going to want to calculate it and determine whether it makes sense using the same formula from above.

Counting Military Time

If you've served in the military, another way to change the value of your pension is to buy back for that military service to add to your creditable time. The DD214 provides a record of your military service. CSRS employees who were employed under CSRS before October 1, 1982, would be required to make a deposit of 7% of their basic military pay plus interest in order to count all that time. However, there's a little loophole here for you. Even if you do not make the deposit, as long as you are not eligible for Social Security at age 62, you get to count your military time anyway. In other words, you get a freebie! You don't have to pay back for it, and it counts toward your creditable service. On the other hand, if you should become eligible for Social Security at age 62 and you have not paid that military deposit back, at age 62, the time for that military service will be deducted from your annuity, and your annuity will be recalculated without those years of service because of your Social Security eligibility. This provision is known as Catch-62, and you want to make sure you don't get caught in it. If there is any doubt about your Social Security eligibility and you want to be absolutely certain that your military time is going to count, you're going to want to make that 7% of basic pay deposit plus interest. If you became an employee under CSRS on or after October 1, 1982, you must make that deposit if you want the time to count.

Under FERS, the deposit required for military service is less; you must make a deposit of 3% of your basic pay plus interest. If you don't make the deposit, you don't get to count the time. In almost all cases, it will make sense to pay back for your military time under FERS. It's going to add to your years of service, it may make you eligible to retire sooner, and it will increase the value of your annuity.

In the past, the advice to employees receiving retired military pay was always that it did not make sense since they had to give up their military retirement – they couldn't double dip. We are starting to see some cases where it could make sense to buy back your military time and waive your military retirement. This is on a case-by-case basis and depends on your rank when you retired, how long you plan to work for the federal government, and your grade and pay at retirement.

Part-Time Service

Part-time service can be confusing for federal employees as they get closer to retirement. For both systems – CSRS and FERS – it works the same. Any part-time service prior to April 7, 1986, counts 100% toward both eligibility and the calculation of your annuity. It all counts. Any part-time service after April 7, 1986, counts 100% towards eligibility as if you'd been working the entire time, but it is prorated for your annuity calculation. A very complicated formula is used to determine what percentage of time you were actually working compared to the actual number of hours you could have been working – 2080, for example, in a year. That percentage is applied to your annuity after it has been calculated.

There's an easier way to do this if you're trying to just calculate it in your head: If you worked part-time for 10 years and you worked 32 hours per pay week, that would be the equivalent of 80% of what you could have been working, and you could take 80% of that 10 years, which would give you 8 years. Let's say your total years of service was 30 years. Rather than having your annuity calculated on 30 years, it would be calculated on 28, because of the reduction for the period that you worked part-time.

That's the simple way to get an estimate; OPM uses a much more complex formula to calculate your benefit. You're just trying to determine if you're in the ballpark when you're calculating these benefits yourself, so that you know what to expect.

Your Federal Employee Group Life Insurance premiums also are affected by part-time service, because the value of FEGLI is based on your actual salary. For retirement purposes, FEGLI is based on the actual salary on your last day of employment.

Part-time employees also pay more for their Federal Employee Health Benefits. They pay a larger percentage of the premium. The government's share is determined by dividing the number of hours they were scheduled to work during the pay period, and dividing that by the number of hours worked by a full-time employee in the same position. That percentage is applied to the government's contribution of 72% made for fulltime employees, so the part-time employee ends up paying a larger percentage of health care premiums. However, the good news is that they still have access to the health benefits. In retirement, all retirees get the same government contribution towards their FEHB premium regardless of whether or not they retired as part-time workers.

The Thrift Savings Plan

"If you would be wealthy, think of saving as well as getting."

Ben Franklin

"A penny saved is a penny earned."

Ben Franklin

These two sage quotes apply as well today as they did over 200 years ago when they were first uttered. If one of your criteria for a successful retirement is income and cash flow that mirrors what you had while you were working, saving will have to be part of the deal.

CHAPTER FOUR

TSP—
Time2Save4Prosperity

Larry seemed uneasy when he sat down at the conference table for our client review. He was within a few months of retirement as a geologist from USGS, and I knew he was double- and triple-checking to be sure everything would go smoothly for his retirement.

As he laid an unopened Thrift Savings Plan statement on my desk, he said, "You open it. I'm afraid to look," as if somehow I possessed a magic letter opener that could erase TSP losses.

"Did you transfer your money into the G Fund like we discussed last time?" I asked, not sure why he seemed so squeamish.

"No," was his sheepish reply, "I didn't want to miss out if the market kept going up." Time and time again, clients come to my office fearful of their TSPs and how to manage them.

How much should I be contributing?

Where should the funds be allocated?

What do I do with my TSP when I retire?

There is no one magic formula for everyone. When you get past the emotional constraints of the TSP, it's a savings plan (notice the name – Thrift *Savings* Plan – not Thrift *Investing* Plan). You're torn between wanting to protect your hard-saved funds and earning a decent return. Understanding the difference between saving and investing can help align the expectations for your TSP.

After two major downturns with another possibly looming on the horizon, TSP participants are understandably queasy. Understanding your options within the plan and creating a strategy that fits your retirement plan can help ease your fears and put you in control of your future.

Tips for Contributing to your TSP

An important Thrift Savings Plan tip for a FERS participant is, do not contribute too much, too soon each year. When their goal is to contribute $17,000 – the full contribution – in one year, some people like to increase their contributions early in the year, so that by the end of September they'll have made the full contribution of $17,000. They look forward to some extra take-home pay for the holidays. If you do this, you're going miss out on your agency's matching contributions if you're in FERS. If you're contributing at least 5%, you're going to get a 5% match each pay period. If your intent is to contribute the maximum, which in the year 2012 is $17,000, be sure it's distributed equally over 26 periods. CSRS participants do not have to worry about this, because they do not get any matching funds on their contributions.

It doesn't mean that you have to contribute the same amount all year; you can change your contribution level throughout the year. You just want to determine that you're consistently contributing at least 5%. Otherwise, you're giving up a valuable contribution from the government.

If you are an employee under the FERS System, TSP is designed to be 1/3 of your income in retirement, although it can represent anywhere from 30% to 50% depending on your career longevity. It's crucial not only that you maximize your savings, but that you also know how to manage your portfolio by making prudent investment decisions based on what's right for you. In the Thrift Savings Plan, the conflict is that it is a thrift *savings* plan, not an investing plan, and yet you're asked to think like an investor.

You're told to be in the market by using the C, S and I Funds. The challenge comes when people recognize, "Well, I'm saving my money – and now I have to invest it, too." It really *is* a savings plan, not an investment plan, so keep the savings piece at the forefront. Obviously, you want the best returns you can get and you want a knowledge and understanding of your options. If you keep in mind that it is a savings plan as opposed to an investment plan, it will help you as you go about making those choices.

A Short History of the TSP

The Thrift Savings Plan was implemented in January of 1988 with one fund—the G Fund. Two additional funds were added in July of that year – the F Fund and the C Fund. These three funds remained the foundation of the TSP until the S and I funds were added in 2001.

For those of you who participated in the TSP from the early days, you'll recall that there were percentage limits on how much of your salary you could contribute. Initially, FERS participants were allowed to contribute 5%, and CSRS weren't allowed to participate at all. Once CSRS employees were finally allowed to contribute, their limits were always 5% less than the FERS limits. When FERS could contribute 10%, CSRS could only contribute 5%. In 2005, the contribution limits changed, allowing all employees to contribute up to the IRS-established limit, making it consistent with private 401K plans.

The total amount in the plan fluctuates (sometimes wildly), but for most of 2011 there was roughly $300 billion in the Thrift Savings Plan, with about 4.5 million participants. This makes it the largest defined contribution plan in the United States. For the first 12 years of the TSP's existence, the stock market, and thus the TSP's only equity offering, the C Fund, went straight up. During that time, the average annual return for the C Fund was 19.41%. What a great way to save for retirement!

Federal employees were lulled into complacency believing they were brilliant investors who didn't have to think about how to allocate their savings. They just had to make sure they were doing a good job saving and putting that money into the C Fund. Now, when asked about how they make their TSP investment decisions, we hear things like, "I just leave it where it was when I started working," or, "Bob in our office is really a good investor, so I just make my decisions based on what he tells me to do." Reminder—an investment strategy that's appropriate for one individual might be completely inappropriate for another; it really needs to be a personal decision.

Many participants also confess to a "don't ask – don't tell" strategy. "I don't open my envelope when I get my statement because I don't want to look at it. If I don't look at it, everything's okay." They've chosen to live in a bubble, hoping that what they don't know won't hurt them.

Younger TSP participants tend to think, "I'm young. I'm going to take all the risk that I can get. The rules of Wall Street say that if I am willing to take on more risk, I will be rewarded with higher returns." But that isn't always the case. One obstacle in investing within the TSP is it's difficult to know exactly how much risk you're taking in each fund. If you look at the average return in the C Fund, which mirrors the S&P 500 Index, from 2001 through 2010, the average annual return was 1.4%. When you're planning for retirement, 1.4% is not enough to cover things such as inflation and taxes.

The TSP Funds

Let's look at the five individual funds in this Thrift Savings Plan, starting with the safest fund and progressing to the riskiest.

The G and the F Funds are the TSP's fixed income funds. The G Fund is the Government Securities Investment Fund, and it invests in short-term U.S. Treasuries that are specially issued to the TSP. Unless you're a TSP participant, you cannot purchase these Treasuries. The G Fund is the safest of the TSP funds because there's no risk of loss. The G fund offers the opportunity to earn rates of interest similar to those of long-term government securities. But again, what are really being issued are short-term U.S. Treasury securities with no risk of loss of principal, because the U.S. Government guarantees payment of principal and interest. Of course, there's risk that the economy will experience inflation, and that your fund's value won't keep up with buying power. But when you're looking purely for safety, the G Fund is the safest fund out of the five TSP funds.

The remaining four funds have their returns tied to different indexes, but they do have a number of characteristics in common. All of them are passively managed index funds, and the current fund manager is Black Rock Institutional Trust Company.

The F Fund is a Fixed Income Index Investment Fund, a bond fund that tracks the Barclay's Capital U.S. Aggregate Bond Index, which was formerly Lehman Brothers U.S. Aggregate Bond Index. It's a broad index, representing government, mortgaged-backed, corporate, and foreign government (issued in the U.S.) sectors of the U.S. bond market. It's comprised of high quality, fixed income securities with maturities of more than one year.

The F Fund offers you the opportunity to earn rates of return that may exceed money market funds over the long term, particularly during periods of declining interest rates like those that we've experienced over the past 10 years. The F Fund has been one of the highest performers of all the TSP funds over the past 10 years with low risk. The main risk in the F Fund consists of nonpayment of interest or principal, or credit risk, which is relatively low because it only includes investment-grade securities, which are broadly diversified. Another risk for the F Fund is prepayment risk, the risk that the security will be repaid before it matures, causing loss to investors of additional interest. Lastly, there is interest rate risk to those investing in the F Fund should interest rates rise, because in a rising interest rate environment the prices of bonds typically fall.

The C, S, and I are TSP's stock-for-equity funds. While they're the riskiest funds, they also have the potential for higher returns. The C Fund, or Common Stock Index Investment Fund, is the second most participated-in TSP fund behind the G Fund. The objective of the C Fund is to replicate the S&P 500 Index, which is made up of stocks of the 500 largest U.S. companies that are traded in the U.S. stock market. This index represents 10 major industry groups, and the stocks in it represent about 75 percent of the market value of the United States stock market.

The C Fund offers you the potential to earn high investment returns over the long term, from a broadly diversified selection of stocks. The earnings in the C Fund consist of gains or losses of these stocks, and also any dividend income that these stocks are paying.

The S Fund is the Small Cap Stock Index Investment Fund. It tracks the Dow Jones Completion Total Stock Market Index, which contains all the common stocks (except those in the S&P 500, which are in the C Fund) that are actively traded in the U.S. stock market. Like the C Fund, earnings in the S Fund consist of either gains or losses of stocks along with dividend income.

The last of the five TSP funds is the I Fund, which is the International Stock Index Investment Fund. The I Fund tracks the Morgan Stanley Capital International EAFE (Europe, Australasia and Far East) Index. This index is invested primarily in large companies in 21 developed countries, not in emerging countries. The earnings consist of gains (or losses) in the price of stocks, dividend income, and have an additional risk due to possible changes in the relative value of currencies.

In deciding where to invest your money in the TSP, you should consider not only returns, but also potential risk. There has to be balance. Of course, everyone wants the highest return possible – but are you clear on the level of risk? Understanding what the maximum loss is that you can handle (otherwise known as your risk tolerance) is important to your development of a personal strategy. It's critical to diversify your accounts in an allocation that is appropriate for you with an eye to your retirement time horizon.

In August of 2005, the TSP introduced their Lifecycle Funds, or L Funds, specifically for participants who wanted the convenience of having their investments allocated for them. The best thing about these L Funds is that you only need to answer one question: When will you need the money in your TSP account after you leave federal service? Once you determine what that anticipated date is, you'll pick the Lifecycle Fund with the nearest date to your target retirement date. What TSP said when the Lifecycle Funds were introduced is that you can be assured that your allocation is professionally designed, low cost, and virtually maintenance-free.

All of the Lifecycle Funds are comprised of the five underlying funds within TSP. Currently, the riskiest Lifecycle Fund is the L2050, which is designed for somebody whose retirement date is anywhere after 2045. Every quarter, the funds are rebalanced, so that they're continually getting more conservative as you get closer to retirement. When you reach the target date, the Fund merges into the conservative L Income Fund, 20% of which is in equities. The allocation does not ever change in the L Income Fund.

Becoming increasingly conservative with your money as you get closer to retirement, with no effort on your part, sounds like a beautiful thing. However, many L Fund participants think that if one L Fund is good, then using multiple L Funds will be better. You'll say, "I have 20% in L 2020 and 30% in L 2030 and 50% in L 2040. I'm diversified in my TSP." In reality, you have no idea what your allocation is – you've simply used the five TSP funds in multiple combinations. The purpose of Lifecycle Funds is to make allocation easier for you. If you're going to use them, just pick one fund.

Another misunderstanding L Fund participants have is a belief that the L Funds adjust for economic conditions. Rocky, turbulent times in the stock market require changes in investment strategy. Unfortunately, the only change the Lifecycle Fund makes is to get more conservative and shift more into bonds as people get closer to their retirement. The allocations were pre-determined back in 2005 when the L Funds were established.

They do not react to what's going on in the economy or in the stock market. In turbulent markets like those we experienced in the first decade of this century, Lifecycle Funds did little to protect TSP savings. This was particularly hard for those who were close to retirement and thought that they were safe in Lifecycle Funds, when they suffered losses right as they were getting ready to retire.

What's Ahead for the Thrift Savings Plan?

What does the future hold for the Thrift Savings Plan? In 2009, Congress passed legislation that included four provisions that affected TSP. The first was the creation of a Roth TSP. This is a great addition to current TSP benefits, because in a low tax-rate environment like we're experiencing now, you can contribute to your Thrift Savings Plan with after tax dollars and have that grow tax deferred, just as in a regular Roth IRA. When withdrawn, all growth will be tax-free. Unfortunately, at this writing, in late 2011, the Roth TSP still has not been implemented, but projections indicate that is should be available in the first quarter of 2012. It might not be as beneficial as tax rates increase in the future.

Another provision from the legislation began in August of 2010, providing automatic enrollment in TSP for new federal employees. If the new employee does not elect to participate in the TSP, he automatically is enrolled to contribute 3%. It's as if they're saying, "Really, you're going to get up to a 5% match. Don't be crazy! Of course, you want to contribute." Employees can choose to opt out once they've been automatically enrolled. If they stay in, their money is automatically invested in the lower-risk G Fund, although they can choose higher-risk funds if they wish.

Another provision was a new survivorship option. Prior to 2009, if a participant in TSP passed away, the surviving spouse had to take their money out of the Thrift Saving Plan and roll it to an inherited IRA or into their own IRA. Under this new legislation, the spouse can choose to leave the funds in TSP with full rights to allocate or distribute as if they were the original participant.

The final provision in the 2009 legislation was the option for the Federal Retirement Thrift Investment Board (governing body with TSP oversight) to create mutual fund choices within TSP. The FRTIB has one primary goal for the TSP and that is low fees for all participants. They have never been enamored with the idea of adding additional funds to the TSP because those additions would typically cause higher costs.

In addition, the FRTIB would have the added responsibility of providing information about those mutual fund choices. Many TSP participants feel that the existing five funds are confusing enough, especially with the addition of the Lifecycle Funds.

If the FRTIB's primary goal is low fees, they have done an exceptional job. The cost in the fund for 2010 was .025% – for every $1,000 invested, your expense is 25 cents! Year-to-date fees for 2011 are even lower at .018%. You would be hard pressed to find an investment in the private market with fees this low. Looking at comparable 401K plans in the private sector, the Department of Labor has determined that the fees are often actually much higher than that, ranging from 2% to 3%.

Magic Numbers

In 2012, the contribution limit for this Thrift Savings Plan is $17,000, if you're under age 50. If you're age 50 or older, you can contribute an additional $5,500. CSRS and CSRS Offset employees don't get any match from the government. If you're under the FERS Retirement System or a FERS Transferee, you'll receive up to a maximum of a 5% match on your contributions. As long as you're contributing 5%, you'll get a match of 5%. Even if a FERS employee isn't contributing anything, his agency will automatically contribute 1%.

If you are under the FERS system, you will always want to contribute at least 5% to your TSP to take advantage of the matching contribution. After all, there's only one thing better than free money and that's free government money!

If you separate from federal service or retire at age 55 or later, you can have access to your Thrift Savings Plan without a 10% excise penalty. If you were to retire at 54 (on an "early-out," for example), you could not access your TSP funds prior to age 59½ without the early withdrawal penalty. Otherwise, you must retire at age 55 or later to have access to your TSP without a 10% penalty.

If they're still working at age 59½, TSP participants can access the TSP for a one-time, penalty-free withdrawal. This provides an opportunity to transfer funds directly to an IRA where an income strategy can be implemented. This allows you to begin receiving income immediately when you retire. You also could opt to transfer a portion of these funds to a Roth IRA, which would allow all future growth to be tax-free. Of course, you would have to pay taxes on any amounts that were converted to the Roth. If you do choose to make that one-time, age-based in-service withdrawal, you can't take anything else out of TSP until retirement. Also, 59½ is the age where you have access to all traditional IRAs or other retirement accounts like 401Ks and 403(b)s without any 10% excise penalty.

The next "magic number" is 70½. If you're retired and not using your Thrift Savings Plan or other tax-qualified accounts for income, when you turn 70½ you must begin taking required minimum distributions (RMD) from these accounts. If you're still working, you don't have to take the required minimum distributions from your TSP but you would still be required to take them from any other tax-qualified accounts. The IRS determines what your RMD will be. At 70½ you are required to take 3.65% of the balance of all your IRAs, TSP, etc. That percentage increases each year, because the IRS would like you to have all of your funds dispersed by the time you pass away.

The final magic number is $1,000,000. Popular financial publications such as *Kiplinger's* or *Money* project that, in order to have a successful retirement, you need $1 million when you retire. This may be scary to even consider. Right now, there are 75 participants in the TSP who have more than $1 million in their account. None of them saved it all there. It was transferred in from large 401(k)-type plans in the private sector, mostly by federal judges who worked their entire careers as lawyers. The good news is that those publications aren't talking to you. They're talking to the "other" people who don't have pensions to count on.

The great news for federal employees is we can put a present value on your pension when you retire. For an average CSRS employee with 30 years of service earning $78,000 a year at retirement, the present value of their annuity is approximately $800,000! That's 80% of the way to the $1 million.

A FERS employee's pension represents one third of his income for retirement. We can calculate the present value of both your pension and the Social Security piece to determine how much you would need in your TSP to get you to the recommended $1 million. Using the same example from above, a FERS retiree with 30 years of service earning $78,000 at retirement would have an annuity with a present value of approximately $475,000. We could run the same calculation for your Social Security. Thinking of each component in thirds, the estimated amount you would need to have saved in your TSP would be approximately $333,000. NOTE: Every situation is different. These are merely rules of thumb for planning. Your circumstances may vary and require more or less savings.

The only way to know your magic number is by planning. To plan wisely, you have to give serious thought to what you want your retirement lifestyle to be and what it will cost. How much income will you need in retirement? Typically, we try to create the same amount of income for retirement that you are currently bringing home prior to retirement. Keeping in mind that there are several deductions that come out of each paycheck while you're working that won't be taken out in retirement (e.g., TSP, retirement contributions, Social Security, Medicare), it is not as difficult as you might think to reach that target.

TSP Loan Programs

There are four things TSP participants control in the TSP while they are working:

- How much you contribute
- How you allocate your funds – both current and future contributions
- Whether you take an in-service withdrawal at age 59 ½
- Whether you take a loan

We discussed the ability to make a withdrawal/transfer of your funds in "Magic Numbers." Another program offered to you while you're working is TSP loans. There are two types of loans. The first is a general loan that gives you up to five years to repay. There's no documentation required – it's your money after all and you will repay it through payroll deduction. You just apply for the loan and the funds arrive within about 3 days.

The maximum that you can borrow is 50% of your current vested balance, up to a maximum of $50,000. Even if your vested balance is $500,000, the maximum that you could borrow is $50,000. The second type of loan is a residential loan. With a residential loan, you can take up to 15 years to repay. It does require documentation requiring you to show that you're using the loan to purchase a property that will be your primary residence. You can apply via a paper application, the TSP 20, or you can apply online (available at www.tsp.gov). The only cost involved is a $50 application fee. The interest rate varies according to the current G Fund rate at the time. Once your loan has been secured, your interest rate is locked in. During 2011, we've seen interest rates as low as 1.675%!

Any time you borrow from your retirement account, there are risks. If making this loan repayment causes you to contribute less to your Thrift Savings Plan, it will have a negative affect on your retirement. Another risk is if the TSP funds earn a higher return than the loan interest rate (which you're paying back to yourself), you're going have less in your TSP at retirement. If the C Fund is returning 8% or 9% and you're paying yourself 2%, you're missing out on earning opportunity. In a low interest rate environment like we've experienced since 2008, this isn't a great concern. Some TSP participants report that the only money they didn't lose in the 2008 recession was what they borrowed!

Residential loans are not considered mortgages, so your interest is not deductible on your tax return. The other concern with borrowing from your TSP is that your loan is being paid with after-tax dollars. You're contributing pre-tax dollars into your TSP, then you're borrowing it, which is not a taxable event. But when you repay that loan, it is being paid with after-tax dollars. When you begin withdrawing those funds in retirement, you will pay taxes on those dollars again.

Reallocating your TSP

You are limited to two inter-fund transfers (reallocations) per month. The only exception to this rule is that you are always allowed to transfer into the G Fund with no restrictions. If the market is in a downward spiral, you always have an evacuation route into the G Fund.

What's really important in allocating your TSP? How should you invest it? How much risk do you hold in your portfolio, and are you comfortable with that risk?

For a more technical approach to understanding TSP allocations, let's get an expert's viewpoint. Before you get nervous and think, "Oh, I'll never be able to understand this," read a few paragraphs of this straightforward explanation on investing and specifically investing in the TSP.

I'd like to introduce you to Brad Kasper, the leading strategist at MyTSPVision.com, an online allocation tool created specifically to assist federal employees with allocating their Thrift Savings Plan. Brad is one of those wicked smart numbers geeks who think topics such as statistics and economics are easy math. And he has a gift for putting that knowledge into every day English. So dive into the next section and be prepared to come away with understanding and a strategy that is appropriate for you.

Before we look at how to create your strategy, let's look at what you won't find here. This is not a "buy and hold" strategy. Nor is it a trading strategy where you're trading in the market on a daily, weekly, or monthly basis (because you're limited – remember the two-allocations-per-month rule?). It is a way to manage these passive, indexed funds into a meatier portfolio for TSP participants. Now, here's Brad...

In my role as an analyst in an investment research firm, I found it troublesome that, with millions of federal employees utilizing the TSP plan, they don't have access to what we define as sufficient data. How do you accurately assess how much risk is associated with each of the funds that are available to you?

For us, the challenge was, could we bring these funds into our systems? Can we come up with a way to track the funds and provide powerful reporting that's available to federal employees? We started by uploading all the historical data back to 1988. Then we added the monthly feeds that are available through the TSP website. At this point we were able to start generating information inside our systems to get a level look into what these funds are actually comprised of.

Today, we not only do reporting on the funds that are available, including measuring the risk associated with each fund, we also provide recommended allocation strategies. There are a lot of federal employees who do not have sufficient information to allocate their portfolios inside the TSP plan, and are unsure about their choices. Our goal is to help them understand what's available to them, with ideas of how to build a meaningful portfolio for their retirement.

There are some common problems that the average investor runs into, problems they encounter because they adhere to outdated concepts of investing. There's a presentation I give to investors, called "What Wall Street Told Us To Do." There are two questions that I always ask the audience. "How many of you have heard of these two concepts? Concept number one: Be a long-term investor." Usually, everyone in the room raises his hand. "Concept number two: if you're willing to take higher risk, over time you'll be rewarded with higher returns." Again, most hands go up.

What I'd like to do is to debunk these myths. The notion of being a long-term investor comes from the "buy and hold" strategy, one that worked extremely well back in the '80s and '90s (think of the C Fund average return of 19.41% during the '90s). But the reason it worked so well was that we had a booming economy and a booming stock market, with more than 1,000% returns on the Dow Jones Industrial Average over that time frame. You could go out and pick an investment, hold onto it, and you'd do just fine. A lot of federal employees who began their investing in the TSP in the late '80s and '90s became accustomed to the notion of buying and holding as a guarantee of great returns. Many of them did very well.

But for the buy and hold concept to work, you have to have two things. First, you have to have time, and second, you have to have guts to stomach all the market volatilities you're going to encounter, in order to get the returns that the markets are generating.

Wall Street likes to give you examples to prove their point. If you're looking at performance of the S&P 500 over a 15-year time frame, you'll see that the average return in the S&P 500 over the 15 years from 1984-1999 was 8.18%. That's a pretty decent return over a 15-year time frame, one that everyone should be comfortable with. The chart goes on to show what happens to your annual return over those 15 years if you missed the best 10 days, or the best 20, 30, or 40 days.

Index	Stayed Fully Invested	Best 10 Days Missed	Best 20 Days Missed	Best 30 Days Missed	Best 40 Days Missed
S & P 500 Composite	8.18%	4.83%	2.26%	.02%	-1.87%

1995—2009

While these are fascinating numbers, they're built around what Wall Street is trying to get you to do. They're trying to get you to stay invested, to buy and hold, because when you move your money away from the market, they're losing revenues.

If a "buy and hold" strategy worked in the '80s and '90s, would it also hold true of a longer-term time frame in the overall market? To answer that, we took a snapshot of the Dow Jones

Industrial Average over 115 years and broke it into two different types of market cycles: bear markets, which is where markets are going down or remain flat, and bull markets, when markets are doing well. Over that 115-year time frame, there were four bear markets and four bull markets. The Dow's first bull market was nine years long, and it was a 148% move on the Dow. The second time frame was five years in the '20s, right before the Depression. Over those five years, the Dow Jones was up 294%. If we were to fast-forward into the mid—'50s, we had an 11-year time frame of 154% return on the Dow. Fast-forwarding again, to the '80s and '90s, we saw 17 years of bull market returns, 1,003% on the Dow Jones Industrial Average. So we have positive-return markets spanning 9 years, 5 years, 11 years and 17 years. And my question is, which of these is the one that stands out?

Over 115 years, the '80s and '90s were the anomaly of bull markets, a period in our history where we had sound economic growth and markets were just accelerating with tremendous speed. You could have thrown a dart at the wall in the '80s and '90s and made 20% off of it. But this wasn't your typical bull market. In fact, it was almost double what you see in the average bull market looking over that 115-year time frame.

Let's take a look at the other side of that coin. What about the bear markets, when markets are going down? The first bear market lasted 18 years, with a return of −4.29% on the Dow Jones Industrial Average. This was 18 years in which you had negative growth in overall markets. Let's fast-forward to the next one, going into the Depression right before the '30s. In that 25-year time frame, the Dow Jones grew 1.69%. If we fast-forward to the next bear market, we get into the '70s. You had 17 years of a bear market with a cumulative return of 0.83%. And if we fast-forward beyond that all the way up to 2011, we actually have been flat for the last 11 years in the current bear market.

Where do we go from here? One conclusion we could reasonably draw from looking at this 115-year history of the Dow is that the average bear market is about 19 years long. Of the bull markets that we've experienced over this 115 years, the '80s and '90s are the anomaly over that time frame. This is the period in which most federal employees started investing, and in which Wall Street successfully promoted this notion of buy and hold; don't leave, just hang with it and you're going to be okay.

We believe that advice is a disservice to today's investor, because it's based on a concept that was created in response to those anomaly years in the '80s and '90s. What we've experienced over the last 11 years is more traditional, with a lot of up-, down-, and sideways-moving markets. Yes, there's a general trend upward – but overall, we are in a more typical market environment today then we were in the '80s and '90s. The idea continues to be promoted that you're going to be penalized if you move your money away, and we saw what happens when you miss the best days in the market – but why doesn't anyone ask what happens if you were to miss the worst days in the markets?

As it happens, somebody did. BTN Research did a 25-year study on the S&P 500.

Index	Stayed Fully Invested	Worst 25 Days Missed
S & P 500 Composite	9.8%	17.8%

1984—2008

The average annual return over that period was 9.8%. What would have happened if we were to miss the 25 worst days over that 25-year time frame? As it turns out, if you'd missed the worst 25 days over that 25-year time frame, your average return would have jumped 17.8%, a little different side of the story here.

First, neither of these tables touted by Wall Street as a reason to stay invested is particularly compelling. It is unlikely that you would capture the gains of all the best days or miss all the worst days in the market (think Charlie Brown). Just because data is measured and accurate doesn't mean you should use it to make your investment decisions.

Second, we think this "buy and hold"/"be a long-term investor" stuff is effectively a self-serving message, generated by Wall Street and utilized on Main Street. It's a concept that was so ingrained in the '80s and '90s that it's very difficult to teach people to think otherwise. When we meet with federal employees, we still see big weightings inside the C Fund, because this is what they've been taught to do. But understanding the overall picture should help you adjust your thinking.

Onto the second myth: If you're willing to take higher risk over a period of time, you'll be rewarded with higher returns. Traditionally stocks have more risk associated with them than bonds, so the implication here is that if you're willing to take more risk inside stocks versus bonds, you'll be rewarded with higher returns over time. The first question should be, "How long do you consider 'over time' to be?" Most investors typically say, "Ten or fifteen years." Wall Street is thinking thirty.

Let's compare stocks versus bonds, using the S&P 500 and the Barclay's Capital U.S. Bond Aggregate. For federal employees, we're comparing the C Fund to the F Fund. When we look at the C Fund versus the F Fund over the last one-, three-, five-, and ten-year basis, on a ten-year basis, the C Fund had a—0.75% return. The F Fund, which is the bond fund, earned 7.10%. This shows bonds outperforming stocks by a little over 7% over the last ten years—the first time in history that bonds have outperformed equities or stocks in this time frame. Bonds are an asset class that has less than a third of the risk represented by stocks. So – you have the F Fund, taking less than a third of the risk of the C Fund with just shy of 8% of annual average outperformance over the last ten years. Where was the benefit for taking additional risks inside stocks in that period?

Am I telling you to put all your money into bonds? Absolutely not. The point of this is to help you to understand the different investments that are available to you. This is why it's so important to understand the risk characteristics associated with the funds. For too long, federal employees have had to live off the research of a two-page snapshot that provides a quick composite of the funds that are available inside the TSP, without access to information on what the associated risks were with the specific funds available to them. Looking at these numbers made us realize that we have to be able to provide better research.

That said, the Thrift Savings Plan has made huge strides. Their new website and some of the tools that they have now are a lot better than they were, even two years ago. But it's our goal to make this understanding intuitive to you, so that we stop thinking about investing the way Wall Street told us to think for so many years, and address how we start building meaningful portfolios.

Once we have research on the funds available to us, we still have the problem of how we diversify it. How do we allocate our portfolio? Most people understand diversification as, *don't put all your eggs in one basket.* Here's the technical definition of diversification: A risk management technique that fixes a wide variety of investments within a portfolio. The rationale behind this technique contends that a portfolio of different kinds of investments will, on average, yield higher returns and pose lower risk than an individual investment found within the portfolio. Diversification is about *spreading your eggs amongst many baskets.* And that makes sense to a lot of people.

But there's a second part to this definition that most investors don't know. The benefits of diversification will hold only if the securities in the portfolio are not perfectly correlated. Typically, when I say correlated, the investor is looking at me as if I'm speaking another language, so let's define "correlation." I'll give you a practical example: I have an older brother and younger brother. My older brother was the leader. Whatever he did, my younger brother  and I would always follow suit. This was wonderful if he was helping Mom carry in the groceries, because then we were all helping Mom carry in the groceries.

But what if he was doing something bad? What happened if he got into the 'fridge and started drinking a beer, and so the rest of us started drinking beer too? All of  a sudden, we're all doing something bad. I would define us as highly correlated kids. The problem with correlation in that situation is that it's great when things are going well, when he's doing good things. But when he's being bad, all of a sudden it's an absolute nightmare.

For an investment example, let's look at 2008 performance numbers. A lot of people invest thinking, 'Okay, if I have large-cap and small-cap stock funds, in the C Fund and S Fund, I should diversify and get some global exposure in the I Fund.' You may have thought that you were well diversified with those three positions in 2008 – until you saw the C Fund lose 37%, the S Fund drop 38.32%, and the I Fund drop 42.43%. They moved in lock step with each other.

So, you tell me – where was the protection out of those three funds? You might argue that you'd spread your eggs out, and that you were diversified. But if you were in a highly correlated position, you did not have a well-diversified portfolio. In fact, the only way to find protection back in 2008 was to go beyond the equity funds and find that protection inside the G Fund – hindsight being what it is. But how often are the F Fund and G Fund talked about in terms of an overall investment strategy? Most people look at the G Fund as an absolutely boring fund. It does the same thing every month.

These days it's looking like a pretty exciting fund, because people want that consistency and performance. The F Fund has never been an overly attractive fund. Back in the '80s and '90s, you saw equity outperform the F Fund, hands down. Investors ignored them, didn't incorporate these funds into their portfolios, and thus were not truly balanced or diversified.

That's where having a strategy comes in. We try to build portfolios with a balanced approach, around a concept that we call *winning by not losing*, which means finding protection when markets are going down. We do not adhere to the "buy and hold" strategy, because too often "buy and hold" actually means "stomach the worst and over a longer period of time, you'll be able to get average returns."

But most investors don't want to be average, and they certainly don't want to stomach the worst. In fact, typically when investors have to stomach the worst, what do they do? They capitulate and hit the sidelines. Then when markets turn around, they don't have any money invested in them. They just suffered the worst part of the downturn, and the money's sitting in cash or in a protective position. When the markets turn back around, they're still at low values inside their accounts. It's a very simple concept; we all want to buy low and sell high. But it's almost impossible to adhere to that, because our emotions prompt us to do the complete opposite. When markets are down we're fearful, and we do not want to buy in. When markets are high, we're happy; we're comfortable, we want to buy in.

That is the trap that most investors fall into and that's the trap that MyTSPVision portfolios are trying to get federal employees out of. It's by utilizing the research; by building what we consider to be more diversified portfolios that are built around the concept of *winning by not losing* over a longer period of time, protecting first and promoting growth second.

Hopefully, that discussion from a professional in market analysis helped provide you with new insights into allocating your TSP.

Creating Income from TSP

Up to this point, everything we've been talking about has been around saving and allocating your TSP. But what happens at retirement? You've put in 30 years working for the federal government. You've done a good job making contributions, and managing your TSP. Now that you're ready to retire, how do you turn that investment into a monthly check?

The Thrift Savings Plan is a great accumulation vehicle. It's easy to contribute through payroll deduction and you have very low overall expenses. The TSP is not such a great distribution vehicle. Remember, the FRTIB's number one priority of low costs? Distribution is expensive and the TSP is not in the distribution business.

To understand the difference between accumulation and distribution from the Thrift Savings Plan, think about the difference between climbing Mount Everest and descending from it. There are strategies that you'll need to employ when you're making that ascent to the summit (aka accumulation) – and very different strategies to use coming down the mountain (aka distribution).

Initially, it's important to consider a safe withdrawal rate. Most retirees express concern that their money won't last as long as they do (they haven't saved enough) and that future market downturns will erode what they have saved. Understanding that market downturns early in retirement can negatively affect the rest of your retirement is useful as you determine your withdrawal strategy.

In this example, we'll go back to September of 2000. Assume your $100,000 TSP was allocated in the C Fund and you had just retired, and you wanted to take $500 a month in distributions. Unfortunately, just as you retired, the market went into a downward spiral that left the C Fund down 44.73% over two years.

Your account value would have dropped to $42,770. The average person is not going to stick it out at this point. They're going to stop taking income, learn to live on less, or go find a part-time job and try to recover. Even without future withdrawals, it would take a return of 133% to get back to the original $100,000 balance.

Understanding the risk of market downturns early in retirement, how can we design a plan for taking income to assure that you're not going to outlive your money? In creating income from your TSP in retirement, you have two alternatives, move your funds to an income annuity established through the TSP with MetLife or utilize your two chances to take distributions directly from TSP at retirement. The second option allows you to either do a partial withdrawal, using form TSP-77, or a full withdrawal, using form TSP-70.

Let's look at those two distribution options. You get two chances to withdraw your TSP funds, so if you take a partial withdrawal, (TSP-77) you only have the opportunity to do that once. If you want to take another withdrawal after that, TSP is going to require you take the remainder out. When you go back to take that second withdrawal you can either take it as a lump sum or as monthly withdrawals.

You need to be cautious with these two withdrawals because they aren't very flexible. If you are taking a monthly amount out of your TSP, and you realize in June that it's really more than you need to cover your expenses, you might want to reduce that amount. When you call TSP to lower your monthly income, they're going tell you that you can only make that change in December (prior to December 15 for January payment).

What if you're taking that monthly income, and you have an emergency? Maybe your car breaks down or you need a new roof – whatever the reason, you suddenly need to take a lump sum out of your TSP. When you call TSP and ask for an additional lump sum from your account – they're going tell you "no." Once you've made the election for a monthly withdrawal, you can't take lump sum withdrawals.

You can leave your money in TSP and take advantage of having low-cost index funds. Just be aware that you're giving up flexibility in distribution, and while options in the private market may be more expensive, they may allow more control and a wider spectrum of investment choices.

An alternative to creating income from your Thrift Savings Plan is through an immediate annuity with MetLife. There are 18 choices for payouts – whether you want a single life or joint life payout, whether you want cost of living adjustments, or life certain payments. Once you send your money to MetLife, in exchange for guaranteed lifetime income, your decision is irrevocable. Because life often throws us a curve when we least expect it, most retirees aren't willing to lock up their hard-saved TSP dollars with the limited options of the MetLife annuity.

What's an alternative for creating income using the two withdrawals that are allowed by the TSP? One solution is a strategy known as sequential income planning. The general concept is that you divide your lump sum into pieces according to the timeframe that you will utilize them. We know that interest rates are low right now, so you don't want all of your funds in a low interest-bearing account. But the money you're going to use immediately needs to be liquid – you need to have access to it. You also want to pay attention to market risk in the short term.

Dividing our TSP (or any other lump sum you want to use for income) into five-year increments allows those funds that you aren't going to use for five or ten or fifteen years to grow at a higher rate of return while you're using the initial pieces.

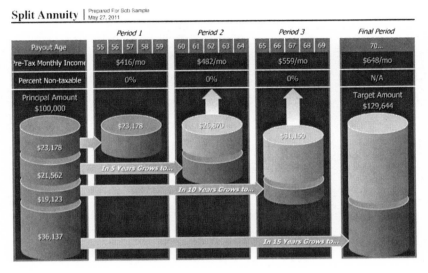

Split Annuity | Prepared For Bob Sample
May 27, 2011

	Period 1	Period 2	Period 3	Final Period
Payout Age	55 56 57 58 59	60 61 62 63 64	65 66 67 68 69	70...
Pre-Tax Monthly Income	$416/mo	$482/mo	$559/mo	$648/mo
Percent Non-taxable	0%	0%	0%	N/A
Principal Amount $100,000	$23,178 $21,562 $19,123 $36,137	$23,178 In 5 Years Grows to...	$26,870 In 10 Years Grows to...	$31,159 In 15 Years Grows to...	Target Amount $129,644

Disclaimer
Report provided for illustration purposes only. Actual values may vary. Tax rates are subject to change and will vary depending upon income. Future tax law changes may significantly affect the after-tax income illustrated in this report. Growth and payout rates may be significantly different than values illustrated. This report does not represent a guarantee of future income.

In this example, the top segment, $23,178, would be left in the TSP in the G Fund. This would provide immediate income of $416 a month. This is secure and would provide that income for five years. The other three segments would be transferred out into IRAs in three investment options.

During the five years you're receiving the $416 in income, the other three segments are growing. Each segment is projected to earn a higher rate of return, because the longer it is before you expect to use the funds, the greater your return should be. As long as you are 59½, you would have access to at least some of the funds in these segments if you needed to make a withdrawal. (You could still take a withdrawal prior to 59½; however, you would be subject to a 10% tax penalty.) If you passed away during this time, all of the balances would go to your designated beneficiary.

Where you'd want to invest these funds depends on your risk profile, but if you're looking at taking a portion of your assets and creating a guaranteed income stream you might consider using guaranteed, safe money accounts. The second segment is projected to earn 4.5% and could be invested in a fixed index annuity or a secure bond-type fund if you were willing to take some risk with this portion.

The third segment is projected to earn 5% while you're using the first two segments and in 10 years will have grown to $31,150. You'll give yourself a cost of living increase, so your income will increase to $559 a month. This piece could have been invested in the safety of an annuity, or in equities if you were willing to take more risk. While you are using the first three segments over 15 years, the final piece is growing at 8%. For this segment, most participants choose a fixed-indexed annuity because of the guarantees it provides for future income. During the time you're using the first three segments of $23,178, $26,870, and $31,150, the final segment would have grown to $129,644 – more than the original $100,000 you started with!

At that time, you could withdraw a guaranteed amount of $648 a month for as long as you live. This is a sum of money and a stream of income that you cannot outlive. If there is anything left in the account balance when you pass away, it would go to your heirs; however, if you live long enough that you've used the entire $129,644, you would continue to receive the $648 a month.

If you compare this to the TSP annuity available through MetLife, where the monthly payments would be $451, initially, you would receive more income than in the sequential income strategy. However, by year six, when the income increases to $486 a month in the sequential income strategy, not only are you earning more income, but you have more flexibility and control over your original $100,000 contribution. Should you decide you want additional money, you have the ability to take withdrawals, which would affect your future income proportionally.

The sequential income strategy is not right for everyone, but it can work very nicely if you do not want to be dependent on the stock market's performance.

Beneficiary Designations

You'll want to be sure to have a completed beneficiary form on file that designates who your TSP goes to if you pass away. The TSP-3 form is available online at www.tsp.gov.

You may notice on the TSP website that you aren't required to complete the TSP-3 if you are passing your remaining funds on according to the order of precedence. The order of precedence has your estate going first to your widow/widower (if living), then to your children; if you have no children, to your parents (if living), and finally to your next of kin. In other words, any remaining balance in your TSP will get to your heirs ... eventually. The easiest way to ensure that your assets go to the people (or charity) that you want to receive them is to use the beneficiary form.

Name both primary beneficiaries and contingent beneficiaries. It's the simplest form of estate planning you can do. Again, if there are no beneficiaries designated on your TSP, it will go in the order of precedence.

Overall Action Steps for your Thrift Savings Plan

Determine your goal. How do you know what your goal should be? Consider how much income you'll need for retirement. Most people try to get as close to their pre-retirement take home pay as possible. This may not be as difficult as it first seems. Remember, several deductions are coming out of your paycheck that will not be withheld in retirement, including retirement system deductions (either CSRS or FERS), Medicare, Social Security (for FERS), and Thrift Savings Plan contributions. Your TSP will need to provide enough income to supplement your annuity and Social Security.

A rule of thumb in determining how much income you can expect to receive from your TSP is approximately $420 a month for every $100,000 in your account. This is a sustainable level, which can be adjusted for inflation throughout retirement. You may also want to consider taking a higher amount in the early years of retirement while you are younger and might spend more. As you age, you could reduce the amount of income you take from the TSP.

Once you understand how much income you'll want/need from your TSP for retirement, you can calculate how much you'll need to save to reach that goal. Calculators are available on www.tsp.gov that will help you determine how much you'll need to save to get to the retirement income you project.

One of the factors you'll want to be sure to consider in addition to a savings rate is a rate of return you'll need in combination with your savings. Establish a strategy that takes your risk tolerance into account. One of the most difficult things to self-assess is your own risk tolerance. If you have saved $200,000 in your TSP allocated among the equity funds (C, S and I Funds), what if you experienced a 30% decline as you approach your retirement? Can you live with losing $60,000? As you get closer to retirement, you may want to consider a more conservative approach to allocating your TSP. You won't necessarily leave it in this conservative allocation for the remainder of your life, but the safety of knowing you won't lose your hard-saved TSP dollars as you get ready to retire provides peace of mind.

Bottom line, have a plan, and follow it – but allow for adjustments that are going to arise from life changes along the way.

Life, Health, and Long Term Care; FEHB, FEGLI, and FLTCIP

"There are worse things in life than death. Ever spend an evening with an insurance salesman?"

Woody Allen

When discussing federal retirement benefits, your pension and the Thrift Savings Plan usually get the most attention. But the lesser-known benefits are equally important, and probably equally as valuable. Among the best is your opportunity to elect health insurance coverage and to choose who you want your carrier to be. You have a variety of good options. Because all FEHB plans are required to have no pre-existing condition clauses, you don't have to verify your good health every year. You can move from plan to plan, which presents a great opportunity for you.

When open season for health benefits comes around every year, there's a collective groan among federal employees; "Ooooh, I have to look through those outlines of coverage again!" But it's actually a great opportunity for you to make sure that you're in the right plan for you and your family. The life insurance coverage is important, because it is an easy way for you to protect your loved ones without having to go through underwriting. You initially get this coverage when you go to work for the federal government, and they don't ask you about your health. Typically, there are open seasons for life insurance every five years; however, we haven't had an Open Season for Federal Employees Group Life Insurance (FEGLI) since 2005. Finally, long-term care coverage is a piece that's near and dear to my heart, because that's actually how I started working both in financial services and with federal employees.

In 2002, when the federal government rolled out its initial long-term care plan, the idea was to sit a group of employees in a large conference room and have a video conference to educate them about the federal long-term care program. It didn't take long to figure out that wasn't going to be the best way for federal employees to make that choice. I started by creating a large database of federal employees who were interested in looking at long-term care, and then sat down with them on an individual basis, one on one, and ran the comparison for them: Here's what the federal plan does. Here's what you can do with private long-term care insurance. Many of those federal employees determined that the private coverage offered better benefits for them. They got richer benefits for a lower cost, and that's how I got my start working with federal employees. Once that original open season ended, I was approached by a variety of people who said, "You understand this long-term care piece so well. You should learn the rest of our benefits and help us with those," and that's exactly what I did. That began my journey to becoming an expert in federal benefits.

CHAPTER FIVE:

Federal Employees Health Benefit Program (FEHB)

Why Can't I Wait Until I Need It To Figure Out How It Works?

F
EHB is the second-best benefit that you receive as a result of being a federal employee, the first being your pension. While you're working, your share of the premiums for health insurance is paid using what's known as premium conversion, or pretax dollars. Many federal employees believe that their share of the premium goes up when they retire. This is not true. The employee continues to pay approximately 28% of the premium with approximately 72% of the premium being subsidized by the federal government.

Even though you are still paying the same proportion, it will feel like your premium goes up in retirement. That's because you pay your premiums with after-tax dollars instead of pretax dollars. If you do three things, you can take your FEHB with you into retirement:

- You have to be insured on the day of your retirement.

- You have to retire on an immediate annuity. In other words, you have to start taking your pension right away.

- You have to have been enrolled or covered as a family member for the five years immediately preceding your retirement or since your first opportunity to enroll.

Five years doesn't mean four years and 364 days. It means five years. For example, Joan was covered under her husband's insurance. When she got within five years of retirement, during FEHB Open Season, she signed up for coverage. She thought, "Okay, everything's fine because I'm not retiring until the end of the December – five years from now." However, that year her insurance took effect on January 4, which meant technically she'd only been in the plan four years and 361 days when she went to retire five years later. Instead of retiring on December 31, when she wanted to retire, she ended up having to work another month until the end of January to have the full five years. If you are enrolling in FEHB at the end of your career in order to take health insurance with you into retirement, make sure you enroll in time to have five full years of enrollment prior to retirement.

You have many great choices for plans. Every year, an Open Season is typically conducted from the second Tuesday in November through the second Tuesday in December. During this Open Season, you can enroll in, cancel, or change your health plan. There is a "no pre-existing condition" clause, which means you can move from one plan to the next, and they're never going to ask you, "Did you have a bad health incident this past year? Is that why you're switching insurance?" OPM requires all of its carriers to allow their participants to move from plan to plan each year.

Depending on where you live, you will be able to choose between some local plans in your area. You'll also be able to choose between six national plans that are available to every federal employee in the United States. As you look at choosing a health plan, you're going to choose how you want that healthcare provided. In other words, what type of insurance might make sense for you?

You might choose a health maintenance organization, or HMO. In this type of plan, you typically choose a primary care physician from a list of physicians that's provided to you. That primary care physician provides all your general medical care, and in many cases must provide you with a referral to see a specialist. Think of it as a silo system where all of your care is self-contained within that silo.

The big thing to remember about an HMO is that there is no coverage for out-of-network care. You have to stay in their service area. You typically don't pay any deductible with an HMO, but members usually pay a co-pay when they receive care from their physician. The tradeoff if you decide to go with an HMO is that you have less choice, but you get to pay less in premiums.

In your area, you may also have something known as a preferred provider organization (PPO), and in that case you don't have to choose a primary care physician as long as you choose to go to a physician that's on their preferred provider list; thus the PPO designation. You can go to any physician on that list, and change doctors whenever you wish.

You can refer yourself to your own specialist. You don't have to stay within network, and it will still cover some of your costs.

However, you have a financial incentive to stay in network because the insurance company will pay more. In a PPO, you typically will have a deductible before your benefits begin, and there will also be a co-pay for each visit that you have to a healthcare facility. This tends to be a little more costly than an HMO in terms of premiums because you have more choices.

Finally, we have the fee-for-service plans that are available to all federal employees across the United States. These are very similar to the PPO in that you choose the doctor or the hospital within the provider network. One difference between the fee-for-service and the PPO is you only receive a reimbursement for the covered medical expenses listed in your policy, which is typically about 80% of "reasonable and customary." You may find that there is a discrepancy between what the doctor thinks is usual and customary and what the insurance company thinks is usual and customary.

The six insurance companies that fall within the national fee-for-service category available to all federal employees are APWU, Blue Cross/Blue Shield, GEHA, Mail Handlers, NALC, and Samba.

Once you choose the type of plan and how much choice you have in the selection of your physician or where the care is delivered, you're going to go to the next level within that plan to decide if you want a traditional plan, a consumer-driven health plan, or a high-deductible health plan. Consumer-driven and high-deductible health plans have been offered only since 2006, so there's not yet a lot of utilization of these plans. That doesn't mean it's not a great option for you. If you choose a traditional plan, you're going to then choose one more level of care between high, standard, basic, or value. Keep in mind that not every traditional plan offers all four of these levels of service.

For example, Blue Cross/Blue Shield offers only Standard or Basic, with the Standard being more costly, offering a few more bells and whistles, and the Basic being less expensive. More federal employees utilize Blue Cross/Blue Shield than any other plan. Does this mean that Blue Cross/Blue Shield is the best choice for everyone? There's a good possibility that the reason so many people are in Blue Cross/Blue Shield is that they have a national network of providers. They've been around a long time, and many federal employees make their healthcare choice simply by going into the break room, finding someone who looks smart and asking, "What do you have? It's Open Season. Help me decide." If you do your research a little more thoroughly, Open Season is a great opportunity for you to possibly save some money and certainly to get coverage that's a good fit for you.

We tend to look at choosing a health plan by simply looking at the premiums and not considering our overall healthcare costs. If you are in, for example, a PPO or a fee-for-service plan, you're probably paying a fairly high premium. You stand to have a lot of things covered and paid for, but if you're really healthy and you don't use any of those benefits, you're paying too much in premiums. You could pay a lower premium and have the same results and benefits, and pay less for your overall healthcare. Conversely, if you choose coverage with low premiums but have a lot of health care expenses, you may pay more out of your own pocket than you would with a plan with higher premiums. It's important that you think in terms of overall healthcare costs, as opposed to just looking at premiums.

When you're choosing between a traditional plan, a consumer-driven plan, and a high-deductible health plan, you should ask yourself, "How healthy am I, and how healthy are my family members who are covered by my FEHB?" A traditional plan is for people who have more significant, ongoing medical issues. If you anticipate multiple visits with a specialist, if you have ongoing prescription needs, and you take two or three prescription medications every month, you may want to look at a traditional plan. It includes higher premiums, but it typically will have lower deductibles and lower co-pays. It will have an annual out-of-pocket limit (which all FEHB plans are required to have), which means that at some point when you reach that spending threshold, you're not going to pay any more that year out of your own pocket.

The consumer-driven health plan (CDHP) was introduced to federal employees in 2006 and only about 2% of federal employees have chosen it so far. Generally speaking, federal employees don't tend to be pioneers. They are more likely to hang back, send someone else in and see if they come back alive (without an arrow in their back). Even though the consumer-driven health plan has been around for five years, federal employees are still waiting to ask a co-worker, "Okay, you tried it. How did that go?"

A consumer-driven health plan is for those who are generally healthy with minor, ongoing medical needs. You may have seasonal allergies or something like acid reflux. If you need any specialist visits during the year, it would be anticipated that you would only need one. Of course, the state of your health can always change during the year, but that's really your whole risk as you make your election in Open Season. You could have a health change during the year, but you're only required to stay in that health plan for one year. You could go to another plan that more closely meets your needs in the following Open Season.

If you have few prescription needs, a consumer-driven health plan can be fairly attractive. It sets up an account that works as a reverse deductible; for example, your plan might pay the first $2,000 of your expenses. You would have no deductibles and no co-pays for the first $2,000 of expenses. After that, your deductible and your co-pays would kick in. If you didn't use more than $2,000 in a year, you wouldn't pay anything out of your own pocket (other than your premiums). If you didn't use all of that money, the funds roll over from year to year as long as you stay with the same insurer. If you only spent $1,500 of the insurance company's money this year, then you'd have $500 to roll over and the next year, they'd pay for the first $2,500 worth of care.

A CDHP focuses on making participants more responsible for managing their health care. It lets you pay lower premiums than a traditional plan, it still has your maximum annual out-of-pocket limits and, if you're fairly healthy, it can be a great way to manage your healthcare costs.

The high-deductible health plan (HDHP) is for those who have no known medical issues. You may have a routine visit such as an annual physical, or if you develop the flu or you fall and break your ankle, you'd go to the doctor – but if you typically don't see a physician other than in those kinds of cases and you have no ongoing prescription medication, a high-deductible health plan might be a great option for you. The big benefit of the HDHP is that it includes a health savings account (HSA) that can be rolled over from year to year. It's one step beyond what you get in the consumer-driven health plan, because these "saved" healthcare dollars are actually yours to spend any time in your lifetime. It acts like a healthcare IRA. You have lower premiums – sometimes significantly lower premiums – than a traditional or a consumer-driven health plan.

Looking at the health savings account, it is the largest benefit of being in a high-deductible health plan. In a high-deductible health plan, you're going to have some minimum deductibles that you have to pay before any of your benefits are paid. Think about the old catastrophic policies where people would say, "I can pay for my doctor's visits, I can pay for my prescriptions, but if I have to have open heart surgery, I want a safety net, I want somebody to help me." That's how a HDHP works.

The HSA in a high deductible health plan allows you to save pretax dollars for future medical expenses. You own the account. When we talk about a high-deductible health plan being less expensive, the premiums are typically less than either the traditional or consumer-driven health plans and you get the advantage of saving tax-deferred dollars to pay for your out-of-pocket expenses. You can get money into your health savings account in two ways. You can put money in up to an annual limit, and the insurance company also makes a contribution on your behalf that's really a rebate of your premiums.

If you look at the premiums for high deductible health plans on the OPM website, you might say, "They're less expensive but they're not that much less expensive." In order to get the whole picture, you need to go to the outline of coverage and look at the reimbursement clause. That will tell you how much of your premium is going to be refunded or come back to you as a rebate directly into your health savings account. You can then use your HSA to pay your deductible if, heaven forbid, you do need healthcare during the year that you didn't anticipate. You also are building an account in which you can have pretax healthcare dollars for the future, throughout your lifetime, so it's a nice way to maximize health coverage for people who are healthy. If you know you have ongoing medical conditions, the HDHP may not be the best choice for you.

Flexible Savings Plan—FSA

During Open Season, although it is not technically a part of the FEHB plan, you're also allowed to participate in a flexible savings account. You can set aside up to $5,000 a year in pretax dollars to pay for medical costs, deductibles, and co-pays. You can also set aside up to $5,000 a year in pretax dollars to pay for dependent care. This might include elder care if you have parents living with you who can't be left alone while you go to work.

Keep in mind that in 2013 the FSA goes to $2,500 a year for medical costs. The other big change to the FSA is that you are no longer allowed to be reimbursed out of this account for nonprescription drugs and medications. If your physician is willing to write you a prescription for Tylenol PM, then you can pay for it out of your FSA.

The one big disadvantage of the FSA is that it's "use it or lose it." The rules of the plan require you to utilize your FSA by March 15th of the following year, so you have to make a plan about how you're going use the FSA.

Another common complaint is that it involves a lot of paperwork; you have to file the claim for reimbursement. That has gotten easier and easier each year. Many insurance companies will actually file with your FSA for you, and the money is deposited directly into your bank account. They're trying to make the process simpler for you.

FEDVIP – Dental and Vision Coverage

In addition to the consumer-driven and high-deductible health plans, also added back in 2006 were dental and vision programs.

These premiums are not subsidized by the federal government. The federal employee or the retiree is responsible for the full amount of premiums, but those premiums are reasonable, because you're taking advantage of being a member of a huge group of people with access to it. It is purchased on a group basis on your behalf, but you're going to pay the entire premium.

Pre-existing conditions *are* included in dental and vision coverage when you enroll in or change from one plan to another, but what you need to ask before you switch is *when?* There is typically a two-year wait for a preexisting condition such as orthodontics to be covered within the dental programs.

As an example, your son or daughter needs braces this year, so you decide, "Hey, this is the year I'm going to sign up for some dental coverage to get some help with that orthodontist."

You sign up for it. You take them to the orthodontist and when your claim is submitted the insurance company says, "Oh, you have to have been covered for two years before we cover orthodontics." Yes, pre-existing conditions are covered and certainly, if their teeth are still crooked two years from now, you'll be able to go and have them pay some portion of those orthodontics. You have to be aware of *when* you need to get in the plan.

You can take just dental or just vision coverage. You can take both. You can take neither. You can move in and out of these plans in any given year. You can never have had either one of them while you were working, and then decide to get them while you're retired. Anything goes; it's much more flexible because the federal government isn't paying any portion of the premium. You don't have to have been enrolled for five years prior to retirement in order to have that access for eligibility in retirement.

CHAPTER SIX:

Federal Employees' Group Life Insurance (FEGLI)

aka – Wanted Dead or Alive

"What happened to my paycheck?" Bob asked. "It's over $200 less this pay period than it was last month. I can't figure out what's going on." It turns out that Bob had celebrated a birthday – a big one – and turning 55 had caused his FEGLI premiums to double while he wasn't watching. "What else have I missed?" he wondered out loud.

Many federal employees make their elections for health benefits and life insurance coverage when they go to work for the federal government. And then they don't think about them again unless a significant change in their paycheck gets their attention.

Let's look at the Federal Employees' Group Life Insurance (FEGLI) next. You must have Basic Coverage in order to have anything else. Your Basic Coverage is your current salary rounded to the nearest thousand, plus $2,000. The federal government pays one-third of the premium, helping to keep the premiums reasonable. The employee pays two-thirds of the premium, or 15 cents per thousand, and the cost of this coverage doesn't go up based on the employee's age. The only time your basic insurance costs go up is if you get a raise or a promotion that causes you to have a higher salary, which results in your coverage increasing.

This option is the least expensive of the Federal Employees' Group Life Insurance coverage. When you come to work for the federal government, if you are under age 35, you actually get double the basic benefit. You get your current salary rounded to the nearest thousand plus $2,000, plus one more multiple of your salary that you don't have to pay for. The current provider of FEGLI is Metropolitan Life, and Metropolitan Life throws that in as a little gift for young federal employees.

You're probably wondering, "How can they afford to do that?" You're not going be under 35 forever, and the odds are in Met Life's favor that you're not going to pass away. Once you reach age 35, your benefits start to reduce by 10% a year until at age 45, that double benefit is completely gone.

You must have Basic Coverage to have any of the other three options, but once you have Basic Coverage you can elect to have:

- Option A, which is a flat $10,000 in addition to your Basic Coverage. The costs for this vary, because it is based on your age and no portion of it is subsidized by the federal government.

- Option B is the most expensive option within FEGLI. It is your current salary, rounded to the nearest thousand. You can have multiples from one through five of that amount. You could have up to six times your salary if you had Basic plus five multiples of Option B.

The cost of Option B coverage goes up every time you have a birthday that ends in a zero or a five (e.g., age 50, 55 and 60). Many federal employees elected this coverage when they first came to work for the government. They were in their 20s, it was inexpensive coverage, so it made sense. "I might as well buy as much as I can. I don't have to qualify by going through underwriting. I'll just take a lot of coverage." Time passes; all of a sudden you have your 50th birthday, and you see this big number coming out of your check, and you're wondering, "What in the world happened?" It's your Option B life insurance premiums.

The chart shows what the cost per thousand is for Option B coverage (effective January 1, 2012), and it gives us a very clear example of how those premiums increase with your age:

Age Band	Premium/$1000/Month
For persons ages 35 and under	$0.043
For persons ages 35 through 39	$0.065
For persons ages 40 through 44	$0.108
For persons ages 45 through 49	$0.173
For persons ages 50 through 54	$0.282
For persons ages 55 through 59	$0.498

continued...

Age Band	Premium/$1000/Month
For persons ages 60 through 64	$1.127
For persons ages 65 through 69	$1.343
For persons ages 70 through 74	$2.47
For persons ages 75 through 79	$3.90
For persons ages 80 & Over	$5.20

This chart reflects keeping the full Option B life insurance coverage during retirement.

- Option C, the final option, allows you to cover your spouse or your minor children. You can cover your spouse in multiples of $5,000, and you can buy multiples of one through five of that. You can cover your children up to the age of 22, in multiples of 1 through 5 of $2,500 for each child. These costs only increase for the federal employee with his or her age. They don't look at the age of the spouse that you're covering or the children, just the employee's age.

In retirement, you decide how much of your FEGLI you're going to keep. Most federal employees choose to keep their basic coverage with a 75 percent reduction, and they eliminate their other coverage. This reduces or eliminates the cost at age 65. The following example illustrates a common scenario.

Your life insurance coverage includes: Basic (equal to your rounded annual salary plus $2,000). You plan to retire at the age of 58. You elected to reduce your Basic coverage by 2% monthly to 25% of full Basic Coverage beginning at the age of 65.

FEGLI Premiums and Coverage

Age Annual	Salary	Biweekly Premium	Monthly Premium	Annual Premium	Accumulated Cost	Basic Option	Option A	Option B	Option C	Total Coverage
56/57	54,124	8.55	18.53	222	222	57,000	0	0	0	57,000
57/58	54,124	8.55	18.53	222	445	57,000	0	0	0	57,000
58/59	0	8.55	18.53	222	667	57,000	0	0	0	57,000
59/60	0	8.55	18.53	222	889	57,000	0	0	0	57,000
60/61	0	8.55	18.53	222	1,112	57,000	0	0	0	57,000
61/62	0	8.55	18.53	222	1,334	57,000	0	0	0	57,000
62/63	0	8.55	18.53	222	1,556	57,000	0	0	0	57,000
63/64	0	8.55	18.53	222	1,778	57,000	0	0	0	57,000
64/65	0	8.55	18.53	222	2,001	57,000	0	0	0	57,000
65/66	0	0	0	0	2,001	57,000	0	0	0	57,000
66/67	0	0	0	0	2,001	43,320	0	0	0	43,320
67/68	0	0	0	0	2,001	29,640	0	0	0	29,640
68/69	0	0	0	0	2,001	15,960	0	0	0	15,960
69/70	0	0	0	0	2,001	14,250	0	0	0	14,250

CHAPTER SEVEN

Federal Long-Term Care Insurance Program, or FLTCIP

The Longest Acronym in Federal Benefits — Whew!

As mentioned earlier, the original federal long-term care program was where I got my start working with federal employees. Over the past 10 years, hundreds of federal employees have come to our office looking for help in analyzing their long-term care needs. The issue most people have with long-term care coverage is it is an emotional topic. No one wants to think they're ever going to end up in a nursing home, which is the worst-case scenario.

From my perspective, long-term care insurance is simply a risk management tool. If you're building a solid retirement strategy, you want to understand everything that is a risk to your assets from taxes to inflation to the risk of needing long-term care. We insulate you from future taxes by looking at tax-free growth investments like the Roth IRA. We look at protecting you from inflation by having some of your assets earning at a rate that outpaces inflation over time. We protect against the risk of needing long-term care by either self-insuring (planning to use your own assets) or transferring some of that risk to an insurance company.

FLTCIP 2.0—This is the longest acronym in federal benefits. The people at Long Term Care Partners, administrator of the federal plan, pronounce it "flitsip." This is the Federal Long-term Care Insurance Program 2.0, meaning this is version two. The original started in 2002 and was renewed in 2009.

John Hancock and MetLife were awarded the original contract. When the contract was renewed, John Hancock was awarded the contract for the second seven-year period. To this point, there has only been an Open Season for these benefits when the contract renews (it's happened twice), so it's not a frequent occurrence. Open Season is great for those federal employees who wish to look at long-term care and have some health issues that might prevent them from getting private coverage. The Federal Long-term Care Program is available to current employees, their spouses or same-sex partners, and retirees and their spouses or same-sex partners. During Open Season, coverage is offered to current employees on a limited underwriting basis. This allows them to qualify by answering fewer questions on the application.

When you're choosing long-term care coverage, you make four choices. You choose how much a day you want your long-term care coverage to pay. You choose how long a period you want it to cover you once you start using benefits. You choose how much inflation protection you want on it. We know that the cost of long-term care is going up at least as fast as the cost of healthcare, so you want to make sure that the benefits you have inside your long-term care insurance will grow to keep up with those costs. You're also going to choose your deductible. This is how long you'll pay out-of-pocket for your care before the insurance company starts paying benefits.

You make the election on how much your benefit is going to cover. You can choose anywhere from $100 a day to $500 a day in $50 increments, so you could choose $150 a day, $200 a day, $250 a day, etc. In figuring out what you'll need, look at what the costs of care are for your local area, and remember that you don't necessarily need long-term care insurance to cover the entire cost of your care. You just want to make sure that you don't immediately have to run to your own assets and start withdrawing them.

You will continue to have a pension as long as you're living. If you are collecting your annuity and you need long-term care, chances are that some of your other expenses, like travel or golf, will be curtailed, so some of that money can go toward paying for long-term care. Your insurance will supplement that.

When you elect how long you want it to pay, you get to choose two years, three years, five years, or lifetime. The average length of stay for a patient in long-term care statistically is two and a half years, so a two-year, three-year, or five-year plan, depending on your family history, might be a good election for you. The most expensive option is lifetime coverage, because the insurance company doesn't know how long they might have to pay. It's very hard for them to quantify that risk.

Inflation protection is something you want make sure that you add to this coverage, since the cost of long-term care is increasing rapidly, and you want to make sure that your benefits are keeping up with those rising costs.

The deductible in long-term care has a really bad name. The marketing department at the insurance company must have been out that day. They named this deductible the "elimination period." If you have not been eliminated after 90 days, then your long-term care insurance is going to kick in. Think of it as a deductible that is measured in days instead of dollars.

You only have one choice for this deductible in the federal plan and that's 90 days. That means you're going to pay for the first 90 days of your care before your insurance begins paying the daily benefit. If your physician certifies that he expects you to need care for at least 90 days, and you need assistance with two out of six activities of daily living – bathing, dressing, feeding yourself, toileting, incontinence, and transferring (being able to get out of a chair and moving from place to place on your own) – you will be eligible to start collecting your long-term care insurance. A diagnosis of Alzheimer's or dementia will also trigger the qualification for benefits, even in the absence of any of the other triggers.

The statistics tell us that about 50% of the population who reach age 65 will need long-term care at some point in their lifetimes. It's kind of a roll of the dice; half of the population will need care and half won't.

If you are healthy today, if you are married, if you live in a state where you might be offered discounts like those available from AAA, it could make a lot of sense for you to investigate private long-term care coverage, because there's a good chance that you can get richer benefits for a lower premium by looking into those outside plans. That is not a knock against the federal plan. It was designed to be as inclusive as possible, so the most federal employees could qualify for coverage. This means that it typically won't be the lowest cost plan.

Entitlements—Social Security and Medicare

"Each problem has hidden in it an opportunity so powerful that it literally dwarfs the problem. The greatest success stories were created by people who recognized a problem and turned it into an opportunity."

Joseph Sugarman

The issues facing Social Security and Medicare are well documented. And yet, they are solveable.

CHAPTER EIGHT

Social Security— Where Have You Gone Joe DiMaggio?

Reminiscing, it often seems that the good old days were somehow easier, better, and happier. Those were the days when people kept their word, you didn't worry about whether the apple pie was organic and baseball wasn't full of steroids.

Today, most people who have paid into Social Security express at least a mild concern that their benefits will be limited or gone altogether by the time they are eligible to receive them. As eligible participants turn 62, they're making decisions to take the benefits earlier rather than waiting to see if they'll be reduced in the future. Recipients are also considering ways to use benefits allowances to their advantage.

Mark is a 62-year old father who had children later in life. His sons, Tim and Eddie, are 11 and 8, and haven't given any thought to Social Security. Neither had Mark, until he discovered that if he took his Social Security benefit at 62, each of his children that are under the age of 18, are eligible to receive half of his benefit! Can you say college fund?

You may be thinking this is unethical, immoral, or fattening, but these are simply the Social Security rules we're playing under.

Baby Boomers want to know: Will Social Security be there for me? How much can I expect to receive? When should I apply? How can I maximize my benefits? And will Social Security be enough to live on in retirement?

Most of us realize that the answer to that last question is "no," Social Security alone won't be adequate to fund your retirement. Having said that, most people tend to minimize the value of Social Security, especially given the current economic environment and fears about Social Security being underfunded. While they understand that they are likely to get *something* back from this system, they think it's going to be a minimal amount and not really enough to count on.

However, Social Security is much more valuable than a lot of people realize. If the past is any indication, people who are retiring today, or even within 10 years, probably are not going to be affected by the likely changes to Social Security in the future.

Social Security provides income you can't outlive. If your monthly benefit is $2,000 and you live for 10 years, you're going to receive a total of $304,000 in lifetime benefits. If you live for 20 years, you're going to receive a total of $673,000 lifetime benefits. If you're fortunate enough to live 30 years in retirement, Social Security is going to pay you approximately $1.1 million in lifetime benefits.

In addition, it offers annual inflation adjustments. A monthly benefit today of $2,000 adjusted for annual COLAs that have historically been 2.8% would provide you with $2,636 in 10 years and $3,474 in 20 years.

Social Security also offers spousal benefits. While a Social Security recipient is living, his spouse can collect half of his benefit if it is more than the spouse's. After one spouse dies, the remaining spouse is entitled to the higher of the two benefits (his own or his spouse's).

Let's talk about Question No. 1: Will Social Security be there for me? According to the trustees from Social Security, the trust fund is on target to be depleted in 2036. Right now, Social Security has an unfunded liability of $15 trillion. In 2016, we'll begin to pay more in benefits than we collect in taxes. So, without changes, by 2036 the Social Security Trust Fund will be exhausted. There will only be enough money to pay out about 78¢ for each dollar of scheduled benefits.

According to the 2011 Trustee's Report, the Social Security Trust Fund now holds about $2.42 trillion in reserves. These reserve funds are invested in specially issued U.S. Treasury securities, and they would be available for paying benefits should revenues fall short of expenses. In 2084, if it remains on its current course, they'll only be able to cover 75% of the benefits that are to be paid out.

Social Security and Medicare entitlement programs represent 8.4% of our nation's annual economy. That's expected to increase to 11.8% by 2035. The projection is that by 2036 Social Security is set to run out of trust funds, which is one year sooner than last year's projection. The Trustee's Report estimates that it would take raising the payroll contributions (half by the employee and half by the employer) to 14.62% to fully fund future needs. Currently, the combined payroll tax from employees and employer is 12.4%.

What are some ways to restore solvency to the system? Some of the solutions proposed include, increasing the maximum earnings subject to Social Security tax, which is $110,100 for 2012. Currently, anyone earning over that does not have to continue to pay Social Security tax on earnings above that amount for the rest of that year. A second proposal is to raise the normal full retirement age, which currently is age 66 for individuals born between 1943 and 1954, or 67 for those born in 1960 or later.

Another proposal is to lower benefits for future retirees, and to escalate benefits based on increases in consumer prices rather than wages. The last proposal is to reduce the cost of living adjustments for all retirees. Federal employees, particularly those in FERS, rely on cost of living adjustments in Social Security to help keep up with inflation.

How much can you expect to receive? Now that we're pretty comfortable that at least some portion of your Social Security benefit is going to be there, how is your benefit calculated? Your benefits are going to depend on how much you earn over your working career, and the age at which you apply for benefits. Social Security is calculated by a formula that includes your highest 35 years of earnings. If you had any missing years, they count as zeros. Your earnings are indexed for inflation and averaged, which becomes your Average Indexed Monthly Earnings or AIME. Then a formula is applied to your AIME to determine your primary insurance amount, (PIA). This is the amount you'll receive at full retirement age.

Example of Social Security Benefit Formula

- Baby Boomer born in 1946

- Maximum Social Security earnings every year since age 22

- AIME = $7,260

- PIA formula:

$$\$749 \times .90 = 714.60$$
$$\$3,768 \times .32 = 1,205.76$$
$$\$2,743 \times .15 = 411.45$$

Total	$2,331.81
PIA=	$2,331.81

Amount worker will receive at
full retirement age (66)

What if you apply for early benefits? Typically, the average age for a federal employee to retire is somewhere between 57 and 62, so should you begin taking Social Security at age 62? There is a lot of discussion that maybe you should, because it might not be there for you if you wait.

But let's look at a comparison. If you were born somewhere between 1943 and 1954 and you apply at 62, you'll only receive 75% of your full retirement benefit. If your benefit is $2,230, 75% of that is $1,672. By applying at 62, you're giving up 25% of your benefit permanently.

If you are penalized for applying before your full retirement age, what happens if you apply after your full retirement age? Using the same Social Security example of $2,230 from above, by delaying until age 70, you would get a 32% increase in your monthly benefit. That's an 8% per year increase. That doesn't take into account any cost of living increases. You want to consider whether there is another asset you could carve income from to delay taking Social Security.

To do the math, start by looking at your Social Security statement to make sure that it's accurate. Go to www.socialsecurity.gov/estimator. You'll need your Social Security number and your mother's maiden name to access your records, and it will estimate your benefits for you. It will show your estimated benefit at age 62, your full retirement age, and age 70. This will help you determine the difference between your benefits and how much you would need to make up out of your assets.

Let's move on and dig deeper into the question, *when should I apply for benefits?* There's not any clear-cut rule, but some factors to consider when deciding when to apply are:

- What's your health status?

- What's your life expectancy?

- What's your need for income?

- Do you plan to continue to work?

- What are your survivor needs?

Typically, the break-even analysis for delaying benefits to your full retirement age, versus taking them at age 62, is about age 77. The break-even for delaying and starting the benefits at age 70 goes up to about age 80. So it can definitely be beneficial to delay benefits if you believe that you're healthy and you're going to live until at least age 80.

The key point to remember when applying for Social Security is that if you apply early, your benefit starts lower and stays lower for life. It's not going to go up when you reach age 66. COLA magnifies the impact to early or delayed retirement. The longer your life, the more beneficial it is to delay benefits. This decision impacts not only your benefits, but your survivor benefits as well. Delaying benefits will give the survivor more income.

Next we'll look at spousal benefits. Spousal benefits entitle a spouse to half the primary worker's benefits. For example, if John's benefit is $2,000, and his wife Jane's benefit is only $800, Jane is entitled to the higher of either half of her spouse's benefits, or her own benefit. In this case, her spousal benefit is higher and would be $1,000.

There are some rules to remember for spousal benefits:

- The spouse will receive the higher of his or her own benefit or the spousal benefit.

- The primary worker must have applied for benefits, but they can suspend to build delayed credits if they're over their full retirement age. That can be a great strategy, as we'll explain below.

- The spouse must be at least 62 for a reduced benefit, or 66 for a full benefit.

- There are no delayed credits on a spousal benefit after the age of 66. If the spouse decides to delay taking spousal benefits beyond their full retirement age of 66, their spousal benefit does not increase like it would if it was their own benefit.

Social Security benefits also are available for a divorced spouse, equal to the spousal benefit if the marriage lasted for 10 years or more and if the person receiving the divorced spouse benefits remains unmarried. You can have more than one ex-spouse receiving benefits on the same worker's record. Benefits paid to one ex-spouse do not affect those paid to the worker, the current spouse, or other ex-spouses. The worker will not even be notified that the ex-spouse has applied for benefits.

Social Security also includes survivor's benefits, so when one spouse dies, the surviving spouse receives the higher of the two benefits. If Jack and Sarah are married, and Jack's benefit is $2,000 and Sarah's benefit is $1,200, what happens if Jack dies? Sarah notifies Social Security, and her $1,200 benefit is automatically replaced with her $2,000 survivor benefit. If Sarah were the one to die, Jack would retain his $2,000 benefit since it is more than Sarah's benefit. The rules for survivor benefits include that the couple must be legally married, a man and woman. Same-sex marriages are not recognized, although common-law marriages are recognized in some instances.

You must have been married for at least nine months at the date of death. There's an exception in the case of accidents. The survivor must be at least 60 to receive a reduced benefit, unless they're disabled; if they are disabled, they can begin receiving the survivor benefit at age 50. A divorced spouse survivor benefit is available if the marriage lasted at least 10 years.

Are there ways to maximize Social Security benefits legally? The answer is yes. If they're available, there's no reason why you shouldn't maximize your benefits. How? One way is to improve your earnings record. Examine your earnings record from your latest Social Security Statement to determine if it's accurate. Are you missing any years? Can you improve it by working longer?

Another strategy is to apply for Social Security at the optimal time. What's the optimal time? It depends on you, and you will want to consider your break-even age, your life expectancy, and your income needs.

Another way to maximize your payment is to coordinate spousal benefits. Depending on the difference in your ages, this is a way to really boost your benefits. Known as "file and suspend," the higher-earning spouse applies for benefits at his full retirement age, and asks that it be suspended. Meanwhile, the lower-earning spouse files for the spousal benefits. The higher earning spouse claims his own benefit at age 70.

For example, Bill and Barbara are both 66. Bill's benefit is $2,000. Barbara's is $800, which is less than her spousal benefit of $1,000. If Bill waits until age 70 to apply, his benefit will go from $2,000 to $2,640. However, Barbara can't claim her spousal Social Security benefit until Bill files for benefits. Their best strategy is for Bill to file for Social Security at age 66 and suspend. This entitles his wife, Barbara, to her spousal benefit, while Bill's benefit continues to earn delayed credits.

Another strategy is "claim now, claim more later." At full retirement age, the higher-earning spouse applies for his spousal benefit only. But his spouse must be receiving the benefit on her record. Then, at age 70, the higher-earning spouse switches to his own higher benefit.

Paul and Irene are 66. Paul's benefit is $2,000. Irene's is $800. Irene files for her benefit at age 66. Paul files for his spousal benefit at the same time. When Paul turns 70, he switches to his own higher benefit and the result is Paul receives an additional $400 a month from age 66 to 70, until he gets his own delayed benefit at age 70.

If you're going to try to do this, remember that the higher-earning spouse may not do this before his full retirement age, so you can't do it at a reduced retirement age of 62. The language to use when the higher-earning spouse applies is that he or she is restricting his application to his spousal benefit. The key word being "restricting." Only one spouse may do this, so both spouses can't be receiving spousal benefits on each other. This can get fairly involved and it might pay to hire an expert advisor who understands Social Security benefits before making these decisions.

Another strategy for maxing out Social Security is to minimize the taxation of benefits. Up to 85% of your benefits may be taxable, which amounts to a surtax for retirees. You pay taxes on your contributions, and it's very likely that up to 85% of the Social Security benefits may be taxed.

If you are married, filing jointly, and your adjusted gross income, which includes half of your Social Security, is under $32,000, your Social Security is not subject to tax. If your adjusted gross income is between $32,000 and $44,000, 50% of your Social Security will be taxed. If your adjusted gross income (including half of your Social Security income) is over $44,000, 85% of your Social Security benefit will be taxed.

If you're single, the numbers for your adjusted gross income must be under $25,000 to avoid having your Social Security taxed. If it's between $25,000 and $34,000, 50% of the Social Security benefit will be taxed. If your adjusted gross income is over $34,000, 85% of your Social Security benefit will be taxed. Most federal employees will pay taxes on 85% of their Social Security.

A good way to minimize taxes on Social Security benefits is to reduce any other income with tax advantaged investments. If you're not using your money, it may make sense to utilize tax advantaged investments, not in municipal bonds, since municipal bonds' interest is included in the provisional income that goes into your adjusted gross income for determining whether or not Social Security will be taxed.

Also, anticipate your IRA. Your IRA is tax-deferred, but anticipate your required minimum distributions. They may put you in a higher tax bracket and subject your Social Security benefits to taxation. Is it becoming apparent yet how important integrating Social Security into your retirement plan will be?

Will Social Security provide you with enough to live on? Probably not, so consider Social Security as another piece of your retirement income, along with your federal pension, your TSP, and any additional IRAs or Roth IRAs that you have in your investment portfolio.

CHAPTER NINE

Understanding Medicare – aka MediScare

There is no other topic that instills such fear in the heart of federal employees as Medicare does. Bob had just turned 65 and his wife, Mary, was only a year away from the monumental birthday when they came to me trying to determine what to do about Medicare.

"This just seems like such a huge decision and if we make a mistake, it could be really costly," Bob worried. Trying to determine whether to take Medicare Part B is a concern every federal employee expresses – depending on how close they are to that 65th birthday.

There are four parts to Medicare. Part A is hospitalization insurance. Part B is medical insurance. Part C is Medicare Advantage, and Part D is prescription drug coverage.

Part A, or hospitalization insurance, pays for in-patient hospital care. It pays for room and board in a hospital, a limited time in a skilled nursing facility, some home healthcare, and hospice care.

You're paying into Part A while you're working; 1.45% of your gross paycheck gets paid into Part A with an employer match of 1.45%. If you're still working after age 65, you continue to pay into it, but will opt-in for Part A, because there's no additional cost. You've paid for it over your work history. There is a deductible and co-pay per day in certain instances, but these are picked up by your FEHB.

Part B covers medical expenses other than hospitalization and prescription drugs. It helps to pay for doctor's services, ambulance services, outpatient services, x-rays, laboratory tests, durable medical equipment and supplies, and some home healthcare. It also pays for some additional services such as physical and occupational therapy.

There is a deductible of $162 a year for doctor's services under Part B. After that deductible, Part B will pay for 80% of this cost. Outpatient hospital treatments are paid the same as doctors' services. Your FEHB covers the deductible and pays most remaining costs after Medicare Part B has paid.

The premium for Part B is based on your modified adjusted gross income.

The chart opposite explains how this works, according to how much you make.

Part B Monthly Premium		
	Beneficiaries who file an individual tax return with income	Beneficiaries who file a joint tax return with income
Your 2012 Part B Monthly Premium Is	If Your Yearly Income Is	
$99.90	$85,000 or less	$170,000 or less
$139.90	$85,001-$107,000	$170,001-$214,000
$199.80	$107,001-$160,000	$214,001-$320,000
$259.70	$160,001-$214,000	$320,001-$428,000
$319.70	Above $214,000	Above $428,000

The initial enrollment period for Part B is a seven-month window that includes three months before your 65th birthday, the month of your 65th birthday, and three months after your 65th birthday. If you're still working at age 65, you can delay signing up for Medicare Part B without having to pay a penalty.

Once you retire, you must enroll in Part B within eight months after you stop working. If you miss these enrollment periods, you incur a 10% penalty on top of your regular Part B premium for each year that you were eligible for, but didn't take, Part B.

As federal employees near age 65, their mailboxes fill with offers for Medicare supplements and questions arise about how to handle the decisions around Medicare. As a participant in FEHB, you are part of the *only* group in the country that can opt out of Medicare Part B. If you choose to sign up for Medicare Part B, your FEHB will act as your supplement. If you decide to opt out of Medicare Part B, your FEHB will continue as it always has.

There are pros and cons to choosing Part B. You may have broader access to out-of-network services and lower co-pays. Medicare will pay the first portion of expenses and then your FEHB will come in and pay the remainder. Pairing your FEHB with Medicare Part B will pay for the majority of your overall healthcare expenses. You will have the additional cost of the FEHB, of course.

What are the negatives? It's costly – currently about $1,200 a year. Blue Cross Standard and Medicare premiums combined are close to $8,000 a year for a couple.

The thing that causes most people to stop and consider whether they want Medicare Part B is that Medicare becomes the primary payer. This means that you must go to a doctor who accepts Medicare, and more and more physicians are opting out of the Medicare program. There are some doctors who do not accept new Medicare patients, and others who won't even continue to care for patients they've treated for years when they sign up for Medicare.

The tradeoff is paying a higher premium (FEHB plus Medicare Part B) in exchange for having all or nearly all of your healthcare expenses paid for, but possibly losing your choice in physicians. If you stay with your FEHB and opt out of Medicare Part B, you save the Part B premium and give yourself greater choice in doctors. But you would pay stiff penalties if you wanted to get into Part B in the future. You also potentially would have to pay more of your overall healthcare expenses out of your own pocket.

The third part of Medicare is Part C, also known as Medicare Advantage. By joining a Medicare Advantage Plan, you generally get all of your Medicare benefits through a private insurer. This is typically an HMO that is paid a flat rate by Medicare to provide all of your care. You must sign up for Medicare Part B to use Medicare Advantage.

Part D provides prescription drug coverage. Private companies provide Medicare prescription drug coverage. Currently, all of the FEHB insurance programs offer prescription drug coverage, so if you're enrolled in the FEHB, you don't need to sign up for Part D. Because FEHB plans are considered Medicare-compliant, if you ever needed to sign up for Medicare Part D in the future, you could during Open Season without penalty.

Medicare doesn't cover your monthly Part B, Part C, or Part D premiums. It doesn't cover deductibles, co-insurance, or co-payments, or outpatient prescription drugs, unless you're enrolled in a plan that provides drug coverage. It doesn't cover routine or annual physicals. Medicare doesn't cover custodial care or cosmetic surgery, hearing aids, vision, foot care, dentures, or dental care.

Nothing about your current medical insurance changes when you retire, except you pay the premiums with after-tax dollars. While you're employed, you pay your share of the premiums with pre-tax dollars. In retirement, it will seem as though your health insurance costs have gone up, simply because you are now paying the premium with after-tax dollars.

The period for general enrollment for Medicare is from January 1 to March 31 each year. Part D enrollment is November 15 to December 31.

People tend to confuse Medicare and Medicaid. Medicaid is a federal program for low-income people, and is set up by the federal government and administered differently in each state. Although you may qualify for and receive coverage from both Medicare and Medicaid, there are separate eligibility requirements for each program. Being eligible for one program doesn't necessarily mean you're eligible for the other.

Medicaid pays for some services for which Medicare does not. If you are eligible for Medicaid, Medicaid may pay Medicare deductibles and Medicare premiums. If you're looking for specific information about enrolling in Medicaid, you should contact your state's Medicaid office, or you can visit the website at www.benefits.gov.

If you qualify for both Medicare and Veterans Benefits, you can get treatment under either Medicare A or Medicare D programs. When you see a healthcare provider, you must choose which benefits you're going to use. You must make this choice each time you see a doctor or receive healthcare. Medicare can't pay for the same service that was covered by the Veterans Benefit, and your Veterans Benefit can't pay for the same service that was covered by Medicare.

You don't always have to go to a Department of Veterans Affairs Hospital or to a doctor who works with the VA to pay for the service. To get the VA to pay for services, you must go to a VA facility or have the VA authorize services in a non-VA facility. You can get more information on Veterans Benefits by calling your local VA office or the national VA information number at 800-827-1000. You can also visit the VA website, www.VA.gov. For more information on Medicare, visit their website at www.medicare.gov.

Social Security, Medicare, Medicaid and Veterans Benefits are too important for guesswork. If you need help, seek out the advice of an expert.

Don't Just Survive— Thrive in Retirement

"Half our life is spent trying to find something to do with the time we have rushed through life trying to save."

Will Rogers

U p to this point, we've focused on the financial aspects of retirement. However, money is actually the second most important piece of retirement planning. Of course, you want to be sure that your lifestyle stays as close to what you enjoy while you are working. You can have more than enough money, but if you aren't healthy or doing the things you enjoy, the money won't matter.

The biggest challenge you'll have in the first few months of retirement is time management. During your working years, your schedule has been determined for you. Someone else determined when you came and left from work, how many vacation days you had and which 11 holidays you were entitled to. In retirement, there's no one to tell you what time you have to get up, where you have to be at a certain time, and what time you have to go to bed. In fact, the number one answer of federal retirees who were surveyed on what they plan to do in their first month of retirement was ... sleep! A part of that is liberating. A part of it is threatening.

There are a variety of things you'll want to consider as you look at making the most of your retirement. We know that those who retire with a plan in place report being more satisfied than those who just "wing it." Understanding the things that are rewarding prior to retirement can help you create a strategy for retirement success – however you define that.

A professional fulfillment assessment is included here to help you identify the things that have had meaning for you throughout your career. Ask federal employees, "What is it that you're going to miss about your job?" and many initially will say "Nothing!" It turns out that within a few months of retiring, there's usually at least one thing that retirees report missing about their job. It might be the people. It might be the complexity of the work. It could be the title and the prestige of your position.

A lot of things that come into play, but chances are that you didn't spend 25 or 30 years in this career to simply say there was nothing you enjoyed about it. By completing this short questionnaire, you'll start to identify what you enjoyed, so that we can consider how to fill that gap in your life in retirement.

www.annvanderslice.com/professional-assessment/

"Wealth is the ability to fully experience life."

Henry David Thoreau

"Being rich is having money.
Being wealthy is having time."

Margaret Bonnano

CHAPTER TEN:

The Yo-Yo Retirement Plan – You're On Your Own

Let's start with a pop quiz to assess your knowledge of retirement and what brings the most satisfaction:

1. Of those who work in retirement, how many do so primarily because they want to, not because they need to?

    A) 12%

    B) 37%

    C) 57%

    D) 68%

2. What is the best thing you can do in your prime earning years to make your retirement pleasurable?

    A) Put in overtime so you can pump up your retirement fund.

    B) Put in time at the gym so you can pump up your pecs.

3. Retirees who have only 401(k)s are just as satisfied as those with only pension plans.

   A) True

   B) False

4. Most boomers want to live closer to their grandkids in retirement. As for those who have sworn off diaper duty, where do they say they'd be happiest living?

   A) In a college town

   B) In a city

   C) In a foreign country

   D) By the water or beach

5. Once you retire, which of the following is likely to have the biggest effect on your happiness?

   A) The size of your nest egg.

   B) Your blood pressure.

   C) The number of people who come to your birthday party.

   D) A hole in one at Augusta National Golf Club.

Answers:

1. D: More than half of those who work for the joy of it in retirement say they're "very satisfied," versus only 16% of those who do it for the money. The lesson: Save now so that you won't be forced into a job you hate later.

Source: Putnam Investments

2. B: Go work out. If you have enough socked away for a moderately comfortable retirement, extra money isn't likely to make much difference. A $10,000 boost in your annual income in retirement raises the probability that you'll be very satisfied by one measly percentage point. Meanwhile, retirees in poor health are 20% more likely to be discontented than those in good health.

Source: Keith Bender, Center for Retirement Research

3. False: Although 401(k)s give you more control over investments, they also bring greater uncertainty, and this weighs heavily on the minds of retirees.

Source: Center for Retirement Research

4. D: Some 49% want to be by the water. Hawaii may be out of the question for most, given that a 3-bedroom ocean-view home there can easily cost $2 million. However, in Dunedin, Florida, a three-bedroom home goes for a more affordable $115,000. With the money you save, you can visit Junior whenever you want.

Source: Money's Best Places to Retire

5. C: Turns out, friends are better than gold. The biggest effect on well-being comes from the size of a retiree's social network. It outweighs even health and money. Those with 16 good pals are, on average, far more satisfied with life than those with 10 friends or fewer.

Source: University of Michigan

"The question isn't at what age I want to retire, it's at what income."

George Foreman

You may have attended retirement classes that lay out how your federal benefits will take you into retirement. The reality is that money and your benefits are the second-most important part of retirement planning.

You might not expect to hear that, but the truth is that once your basic needs are met, having more money won't necessarily make you happier. What you will do and who you will be in retirement are much more important than the dollars.

Some things to consider: Could you survive another market downturn like the one we saw in 2000 through 2002? Or 2008? Or even the Great Depression, especially if you were in or close to retirement? Are you secure that you will have enough income to be able to maintain your desired standard of living throughout your retirement? We're talking about income security. This is not your parents' retirement. For many years, the retirement system was simple and worry-free. The employee was not responsible for the plan's investment decisions, which resulted in a lack of anxiety. A retirement meant that the retiree would receive a pension check, guaranteed for life. This type of plan is called a "defined benefit plan," and is what your CSRS and FERS pensions are.

Under the new retirement system, you're on your own, also known as the "yo-yo" retirement plan. With the implementation of FERS in 1987, federal employees became more responsible for managing their own retirement income. It's not better or worse than CSRS – it's just different, and it put more of the retirement responsibility on you. In addition to defined benefit pensions, your parents could ladder bonds and CDs. Interest rates didn't fluctuate dramatically and typical yield curves prevailed – 5-year CDs paid more than 3-year CDs, which paid more than 1-year CDs. But for most retirees today, this method will not create enough income or liquidity to meet their retirement income needs.

Do you want your retirement success to be dependent on how the stock market is doing? Do you want your retirement income to be dependent on what the Federal Reserve Board decides to do? Do you have a plan so that taxes will not take a bite out of your retirement?

Hopefully, you'll have a long life in retirement. Statistics (from the *US Annuity 2000 Mortality Table Society of Actuaries*) tell us that, for a couple who are both 65 today, there's a 50% chance that one will live to age 90. There's a 25% chance that one will live beyond age 95.

In planning for retirement, you must anticipate rising healthcare costs and attend to inflation's impact on your future buying power. Taxes may take a larger bite out of retirement income, and most retirees recognize how an extended illness or the need for long-term care could affect the future.

There are some common misconceptions about retirement income. The first, created by Wall Street, is the idea that a secure retirement comes from dividends and interest. The reality is that there's no certainty that Wall Street will be able to provide this. When creating retirement income solely this way, many retirees are risking short-changing their lifestyles.

If the years leading up to retirement are hazardous, the years immediately *following* retirement can be even more dangerous because of the timing factor. Any adversity in the early years of retirement has a negative impact on the remaining years.

The importance of this is illustrated in the following example: Joe Smith is 62 and retiring this year. He has savings of $250,000 and plans to withdraw 5% of his account value each year, adjusted annually for 3% inflation. We'll assume his portfolio will average a 6% rate of return over the next 30 years.

Three years earlier, Mary Jones had retired at the age of 62 with $250,000 in savings. Like Joe, Mary planned to withdraw 5% of her account value each year, adjusted annually for 3% inflation. We'll assume she also enjoyed an average annual return of 6% for a 30-year period.

Is it safe to assume that Joe and Mary had the same amount of money at the end of their 30-year period? No, because of something called the sequence of returns. Here's the outcome: Joe was completely out of money by the age of 77; 15 years into retirement and flat broke. Mary did rather well, and had an account balance of $432,000 after 30 years of retirement. The order that the returns occur is important to understand – and also completely out of your control.

How did this happen? Unfortunately, Joe had bad luck. Upon his retirement, the stock market went through a downturn. The first year, his account dropped by 18%, followed by a 13% drop in the second year, and an 11% drop in year three.

Mary was luckier with her portfolio. When she decided to retire at the age of 62 with $250,000 in her retirement account, she experienced three positive years early on. Year 1, her portfolio increased by 15%, year two, an increase of 6%, and year 3, an 11% rate of return. While her declines were pretty severe in the later years, the outcome still left her with $432,000 after 30 years, where Joe was out of money by his year 15. Yet, both Joe and Mary's portfolios had the same annualized average return of 6% over thirty years!

Another common misconception is that if your portfolio averages an annual return of 6% and your withdrawal rate is 5%, you don't ever have to worry about running out of money. While this seems logical in your mind, the reality is that the sequence of returns will determine how much you have in your portfolio.

You may think that you can continue to invest in the same way that you did while you were working. The reality is that, during the distribution stage (when you start using your hard-saved dollars for income), your portfolio should have protection strategies to overcome volatility, especially in the early years. A perfect example is what happened in 2000-2002. If you had an account value of $100,000 and you were in the TSP C fund from September 2000 till September 2002, your account value would have dropped to $55,270. In order to get back to the $100,000 mark, you would need an 81% rate of return. In this example, if you had held on and stayed in the C fund, you would have made that back up.

What if you're taking a $500 per month distribution? If you go through the same market downturn from September 2000 through September 2002, now your account value has dropped all the way to $42,770. You still need that $500 a month to meet your fixed expenses. What are you going to do? The likelihood of your account running completely down to zero is pretty high. It's critical to understand that when you're taking income, you have to change your perspective. You have to plan much differently for distribution than you did when you were in the accumulation phase.

Another obstacle for creating income in retirement is determining whether TSP is the best choice for taking income. The reality is that it depends on the individual circumstances. For some people, the TSP can be the best choice for taking income. For others, it's not.

If you are okay taking a pre-determined amount of income from TSP, if you're comfortable with the allocation of the funds, and if you can live within the restrictions that TSP has regarding withdrawals, then you might be perfectly comfortable leaving it in TSP. It is the inflexibility in the withdrawal rules that makes most TSP participants choose to transfer their funds from the TSP to an IRA at retirement. Remember, the TSP Board's priority of low costs? Multiple distribution options increase costs. The TSP is a great accumulation tool, but the TSP is not in the distribution business.

If you were taking $1,000 a month in withdrawals directly from TSP, and your car broke down, you couldn't call TSP and say, "Send me a check for $15,000. I need to get a new car." Once you are taking monthly payments, you can't go back and take a partial withdrawal. Your only alternative at that point would be to wait until December when you would be allowed to change your monthly income amount. However, you still couldn't get a lump sum amount.

It works the same way if you're taking income and you want to take less income during the year. You get to the middle of the year and realize that taking the same amount of income for the remainder of the year will put you into a higher tax bracket, which affects your Social Security and your Medicare premium. You can't call TSP and ask them to stop your automatic payments for the rest of the year. Once you're taking monthly income directly from TSP, you are only allowed to make changes in December.

The decision whether or not to stay in TSP depends on your particular circumstances and needs. The funds are index funds and they're very low cost, but you have to be willing to live within the restrictions. For some, it might better to move your TSP to an IRA and look at other investment options. It's important that if you utilize strategies outside the TSP, you're doing it for the right reasons. If you believe it's a more suitable investment strategy, and you will have more flexibility in withdrawing from your TSP, it can be a great decision. It really depends on the individual situation.

You may have heard the "rule of thumb" that you'll need 70% to 80% of your pre-retirement income for retirement. The next question is, "70% to 80% of what? My gross pay? My net pay?" The best way to find out is to complete a full analysis of your income and expense needs and goals, which will give you an accurate determination of your income need. Often, federal employees are able to have the same amount of income in retirement that they were bringing home prior to retirement. Additionally, you need to take other costs into account: inflation, taxes, and the rising costs of healthcare, which are outpacing the overall rate of inflation. It's important to look beyond the first couple of years of retirement to make sure that your income needs are going to be met for the long term.

What can you do now to resolve these roadblocks and others that may arise along the way? First, recognize that the biggest fear retirees express – running out of money—doesn't change. The way you manage the process of creating income has changed, putting more and more of the responsibility on you. You need to be sure that your TSP allocations are right both while you're working and once you retire. You have to make certain that you will have enough income throughout your retirement. It's not the government's job to do that.

You have to analyze your long-term care options, because poor planning for long-term care can wipe out all your goals for your retirement, not only financially but also with the emotional strain it creates on you and your family.

Utilize the tools that are available for creating income. There is a wide variety of tools to ensure you're getting income sufficient to meet your fixed expenses. And whether you work with a financial expert or do it yourself, make sure you utilize the tools that are available to you in managing your TSP for creating income for life.

Having started this section telling you that money is the second most important piece of retirement planning, the first part of this section has been about income and money. Now let's move into the really important topics, like, "Where will you live in retirement?"

CHAPTER ELEVEN

Back to the Future
What Will Your Retirement Look Like?

Where to Live?

Although a lot of people report that they are going to stay right where they are after retirement, about an equal number report that they're going to move and live somewhere else. Among the things that you'll want to consider when you're deciding where to live in retirement is the lifestyle that you're looking for. Do you want a fast-paced lifestyle, the opportunity to go to arts or educational events, a very busy community – or are you looking for a more laid-back lifestyle? Are you looking for a place where there are lots of outdoor activities?

You want to make sure that you're matching up your expectations with what the community you choose actually offers. You'll also want to consider the healthcare options within that community. You're going to have great health benefits to take with you into retirement, but you want to be sure that you'll have access to the kinds of health delivery systems that partner nicely with your health insurance.

You'll also want to know about the housing and the real estate market in these communities. Is it going to cost you more to live in the place you want to live in retirement? Many people assume that they're going to live in a place that will cost them less, that the housing they're planning to relocate to will be less expensive than where they're starting out. In recent years, that hasn't always been the case, but it is highly dependent on the actual location you're considering.

Climate is usually an important consideration when deciding where you're going to move. Think about whether you want to be in a place that has four seasons, versus a place where it's warm year-round. Why do you think so many retirees end up in California and Florida?

What are the taxes like? Some states – Alaska, Florida, Nevada, New Hampshire, South Dakota, Tennessee, Texas, Washington, and Wyoming – actually have no state income tax. (New Hampshire and Tennessee don't tax wage income, but they do tax interest and dividends.)

When you consider a state that has no income tax, you may be thinking, "Oh, well, at least I'll have a little extra money to spend there." However, remember that every community has certain fixed expenses for things such as public safety, water, streets, etc. One way or another, these expenses have to be paid, whether it's through a state income tax, through sales tax, or through property taxes. The states that have no sales tax tend to have higher property taxes. Ultimately, you're probably going to pay about the same amount in total taxes.

There are many ways you can find the best places to live in retirement. If you simply Google "best places to live in retirement," you'll get a long list of possibilities. *Kiplinger's* magazine and *Money* magazine both put out yearly publications on this topic, as does Yahoo, so you can review their criteria and match them against your needs and wants.

For 2010, the "best places to live" were listed as: Durham, North Carolina; Hanover, New Hampshire; Lexington, Kentucky; Prescott, Arizona; Bellingham, Washington; and Boise, Idaho. Clearly, these are very diverse locales, so keep in mind that their criteria might not be the same as your criteria. It's just a place to start.

To Work, or Not to Work?

Some baby boomers say that they're going to get a job in retirement. They say, "When I stop working for the federal government, I'm going to get a 'fun job'." There are several reasons federal employees decide to work in retirement. They may need the money to supplement the income from their federal pension and what they can create from their TSP and Social Security, if they have access to it. They may want to wait to take their Social Security until later when the value of their Social Security benefit is higher. So they decide to work in those interim years after retiring from the federal government doing a part-time job, or even something completely different from what they were doing.

Some people come back to work for the federal government as contractors, or become consultants doing exactly the kind of work they were doing when they were federal employees. Consulting is an interesting option. A lot of private companies are interested in hiring federal employees who have the experience to help them navigate the complexity of the federal government from the inside.

How do you find the best job in retirement? If you're thinking about simply leaving the federal government and going to work in another full-time job, you might be better off staying where you are. If you are really not comfortable or not happy in the agency you're in, it may be possible to move to another agency. If you're going to continue to work a full-time job, it could be challenging for you to find a job that would offer you the same pay, continue to increase your pension, plus allow you to add to a plan like a Thrift Savings Plan.

You can look for a part-time job in either your current profession or something new. You might work as a temporary employee, especially if you're not sure just what it is that you want to do. Some employers look to bring on temporary seasonal workers, so it gives you a chance to try before you buy. Perhaps you've always thought you'd love to work in a pet store, in the flower shop or at the golf course. This gives you a chance to go in and try it out, and find out whether that's a good fit for your personality.

You can also use government and community programs. A variety of resources are out there for retirees to help them get back into the workforce, or to help them remain useful members within the community.

Some people simply don't feel fulfilled unless they're contributing something by working. Many federal employees say, "I've been working since I was 14 or 15 years old and the idea of just stopping because I'm eligible to retire feels very uncomfortable." We know that people who can ease into retirement – who go from working 40 hours a week to 32, or down to 24 – make that transition much more easily as opposed to going from 40 hours a week to zero.

Another reason that federal employees may want retirement jobs is because their social life is connected to their work life, and they're used to having most of their friends in the workplace. They fear a different lifestyle, and put off that shift to retirement because they aren't sure what it's going to look like. Some federal employees spend their whole careers watching the countdown clock – that gently ticking marker that tells them how many years, months, and days they have until retirement. They've been waiting for 30 years for this event. Others didn't start to pay attention to retirement until they were within a few months or a year of it.

While hitting retirement's finish line can be very exciting, for some people it feels more like a cliff because it can be a little scary. You don't know what's on the other side of that line. You know what it's like to get up and go to work every day when someone else is setting your schedule. When you're setting your own schedule and you get to decide what you're going to do, it becomes a little more daunting.

For a Good Cause—Volunteering

One of the top things that retirees report that they want do is to volunteer. When considering volunteering, we encourage you to volunteer wisely. Time management is such an important issue to deal with in retirement (especially early in retirement). You're now the master of your own clock. No one is telling you when you have to get up, when you have to be at work, how many days off you get, or when your holidays are, so now you have the opportunity and the responsibility to manage your time. If one of the things you determine that you want to do in retirement is to volunteer for a cause that's important to you, make sure that you take time management seriously. Nonprofit organizations are struggling mightily for contributions and to get good people to work in their organizations. When you put your name out there as being available to work for them, you will literally have your calendar filled before you know what's hit you. They will line up to take advantage of your availability. That may end up with you saying, "I feel like I'm working 40 hours a week," because you find yourself overwhelmed with volunteer opportunities.

You probably have heard some of your retired friends, neighbors or family members say, "I'm busier now than when I was working." Hopefully because you're looking at this plan ahead of time, you're going to take the opportunity to consciously manage your time, so that you don't end up overwhelmed. Don't let someone take your hard-earned downtime away from you.

Take the time to identify what causes and issues are important to you. Consider what skills you have to offer. One of the things you'll want to do, as you determine those agencies or nonprofit organizations that you want to work with, is put together a little résumé, not necessarily based on all of your work experience but on the things that you would like to do in the volunteer realm. If you simply go in and say, "I have time to volunteer," you could end up stuffing and licking envelopes and not enabling the non-profit to take advantage of your skills.

It's a common mistake for people not to let the volunteer organization know what skills they have, and the way that they can best serve the organization. You have to do a little bit of marketing, unless, of course, you're happy stuffing envelopes. If you're happy to become the Jack of all Trades or the Gal Friday for an organization, that's fine, but if you have specific things you want to do, you have to make sure that you let them know that. If you're willing to learn something new, let the volunteer organization know that, as well. Combine your goals of learning to do something new with the time that you have on your hands to help those organizations out.

Finally, make sure that you don't overcommit your schedule. You want to leave yourself time to enjoy your retirement.

"Find something that you're really interested in doing in your life, and commit yourself to excellence. Do the best you can."

Chris Evert

Some of the places that you can consider volunteering? Look at the familiar nonprofits, of course, but also think outside the box. Consider virtual volunteering. You can do many things online. If you have great computer skills, there are things that you can do right at home to help an organization, without ever having to leave home.

Look at daycare centers, public schools or your local library. As budgets for these organizations get cut, they are desperate for people to help them. If you have great skills in math, for example, you could help tutor middle school or high school kids in trigonometry or calculus. It's great for you, because it's good for your brain, and teaching keeps those neural pathways open. It's also great for the kids to get that one-on-one attention and have the opportunity to get help in a smaller setting.

Look at animal shelters, museums and galleries, Neighborhood Watch, and community theaters. Look at the airport – many airports utilize volunteers to work as greeters and answer travelers' questions.

Meals on Wheels always needs drivers. Soup kitchens need servers, stockers, sometimes even seasonal help in gardens. If you have a talent for singing or playing a musical instrument, you might look at the community choir or the community symphony, or consider volunteering to entertain at a retirement home. There are more opportunities than you have hours in the day, so having a plan prior to retirement can help you to be selective in the beginning.

> **TIP:** Wait six months before you make a firm commitment to take on any of these things. That doesn't mean that you're not going to take an opportunity to be part of a fundraising committee or a special event, but if you can go six months so you're comfortable in your schedule and you can see what kind of time you really have, you'll be more successful in managing that time.

Be A Life-Long Learner

Federal employees commonly make a passion out of continuing to learn while they're in retirement. What are those things that you want to make sure that you're involved in, and that you're interested in learning about? It's proven that those who are lifelong learners have a greater sense of optimism and a lower chance of dementia, so whatever your interests are, now is the time to dive in. If you have always wanted to learn more about philosophy, wanted to take a cooking class, or learn a foreign language, now's the time.

Maybe you're interested in classical literature. Maybe you just want to get up to speed on computers and the latest technology. Lots of people take up genealogy, and research their family history. You might enjoy an art appreciation class, or learning more about wine. There are endless possibilities to continue your learning and promote your lifelong learner title.

Put on Your Traveling Shoes

Once they're all caught up on their sleep, the next thing retirees nationwide report that they really want to do is … travel. How can you do that on a budget and make the most use of your travel dollars?

Part of the fun of traveling, if that is something that you want to do, is deciding where you want to go – and the sky should be the limit! Don't eliminate something from this initial list of where you'd like to travel, whether it's Africa, Europe, Disneyworld, New York City, the Caribbean – put it on your list. Don't eliminate it simply because you think, "That might be too expensive," because there are lots of great resources to help you manage the costs.

Remember that, in the past, the times that you were able to travel and go on vacation were also the times that everyone else was able to go on vacation. That translates to higher airfares, higher hotel rates, and bigger crowds. But now, unlike those people who are still working, you have the gift of time. You can choose when you're going to go, and traveling in the low season can make your trip much less expensive, even to very nice places. On the following page is a web address that will take you to a great travel resource guide.

www.annvanderslice.com/blog/discount-travel-websites/
Password is Travel Discount

Included in this travel resource guide are money-saving tips to help you vacation better. How do you get the best deals on golf? How do you get the best deals on theater tickets, if you're going to New York or Las Vegas? There are lots of great resources to help you figure out where the best deals are on everything, from your actual travel plans to where you're going to eat dinner, so check it out and make those travel dreams come true.

Another way to save money on outings is to buy entertainment coupon books. You probably have neighborhood kids who come to your door to sell you entertainment books and you're thinking, "I don't want to use coupons," but these are actually a great bargain. You'll find that they will pay for themselves 10 times over or more. There are some other great resources online, too, for saving money on dining out. Restaurant.com and Groupon are both popular, and you can use these same resources when you're traveling, too.

Thinking About Retiring Abroad?

About 5% of federal pre-retirees ask questions such as, "What happens to my federal pension if I retire abroad?" or "What happens with my health coverage if I retire abroad?" As the cost of retirement continues to increase in the U.S., more and more people are looking at those places that are less expensive, like Mexico, Costa Rica, South America, or Southeast Asia. Many great travel books now provide advice on the best places to live abroad on low incomes.

Some people say they're going to join the Peace Corps now that they've retired, which is a very inexpensive way to live abroad if you're interested in living a simple lifestyle within a foreign community that combines volunteer work with a travel experience.

A couple of the issues around retiring abroad: Your health coverage typically will cover you on a limited basis while you're abroad. You probably are going to have to get some other type of coverage, depending on whether you are considering becoming an ex-patriot and keeping your U.S. citizenship, or whether you obtain dual citizenship.

If you're no longer using your federal health benefits, and you're going to use the health benefits in the country where you're going, you want to make sure that you suspend your FEHB coverage. Don't cancel it. You don't have to pay for it while it is suspended. Use the benefits of the country you're in, then if you ever want or need to come back to the United States, you can simply reinstate those health benefits.

For Better Or Worse, but Not For Lunch

A common question from couples as they move into retirement is, "Should we retire together?" Consider when the last time was that you spent 24 hours a day, 7 days a week, 365 days a year with your spouse. That would probably be never, and now you're literally going to be thrown together, full-time, in your house. By talking through some of these things together ahead of time, you can determine that you don't always have to be right next to each other, doing the same thing. Make sure that you're communicating both the positive aspects of spending time together, as well as your frustrations.

Have a purpose for what you're going to do together. Create some structure around those things that you're going to do together, but you also each need to have your own community. Be an individual. Don't simply become a part of "we." You still want to have your individuality.

Work on a budget together, because you may have very different ideas about how you're going to spend those retirement dollars that you'll be living on now. Explore interests together that you didn't have time for prior to retirement. Making a plan ahead of time will help resolve a lot of those conflicts before they ever happen.

Ron and Loretta decided that they were going to retire together. They were both federal employees and they were both high performers in their jobs, so I was a little concerned about the two of them alone together for 24 hours a day, but they did a great job. When they retired, they decided together that they each wanted to do a little consulting on the side, which allowed them to spend time away from each other and still be that independent person that they were while they were working, but with fewer hours. It also gave them a few extra bucks early in retirement, which allowed them to travel and take some trips together that they'd always wanted. After the first year in retirement, they reported, "We made it work!"

Make Your Bucket List

This chapter started with a professional fulfillment assessment about looking back through your career and identifying the things that you enjoyed during that time. Now we're going to do another worksheet about things you've always wanted to do and things that you may already be doing that you would like to do more of. You might have started doing them before you retired, but you want to make sure that you continue them in retirement. It's called, *Dream Forward,* but it's really your "bucket list."

If you remember the movie of that name that starred Jack Nicholson and Morgan Freeman, this odd couple was forced into making a bucket list of all the things they wanted to do before they died, because they both had terminal illnesses. The premise of the movie was, of course, don't wait until you're diagnosed with something awful to do the things you really want to do.

You get to determine which of these things you're going to make sure you don't miss along the way; a to-do list prior to retirement.

www.annvanderslice.com/blog/dream-forward/

Get Organized

People who go into retirement with a plan report being 60% more satisfied at the end of their first year of retirement than those who had no plan and just decided to wing it.

Make sure that all your beneficiary forms are updated. This is part of the process of putting all your important papers in one place. Review your estate plan if you haven't done so within the last three years.

"Fast is fine, but accuracy is everything."

Wyatt Earp

If you don't have a computer at home, you may want to consider getting one because it's like a lifeline to the world. You may not have needed one at home because you've used the computer at the office, but what you'll find is that you'll feel pretty isolated without it.

Make sure you have your emergency fund created. You want to have six months' worth of expenses in this emergency fund. Remember that initially you're not going to get your full retirement amount from OPM. There will be a few months' lag time in which you're only getting a partial payment, so you want to make sure that worrying about money isn't the first thing you end up doing in retirement. Prepare a budget, so you have an expectation of both what's coming in and what you're going to spend.

If you plan to move, have a strategy for doing that. When are you going to move – immediately after you retire, or at some point down the line? How are you going to put your house on the market?

All of these things need to be part of a list, which is an important part of your retirement strategy. In more than 10 years of helping federal employees retire, never, not once, has someone come back to me and said, "I shouldn't have retired. I wish I would've worked longer." There can be some challenges in figuring out what you're going to do, but those challenges are not so daunting that you'll wish you were still on the job.

You've made it to the end! Hopefully, this book has helped you gain insights, learn more about your benefits, and be a little less intimidated about planning for retirement.

"Twenty years from now, you will be more disappointed by the things you didn't do than by the ones that you did do, so throw off the bow lines, sail away from the safe harbor, catch the trade winds in your sails. Explore, dream, discover."

Mark Twain

How can you use this book?

MOTIVATE

EDUCATE

THANK

INSPIRE

PROMOTE

CONNECT

Why have a custom version of *FedTelligence?*

- Build personal bonds with customers, prospects, employees, donors, and key constituencies
- Develop a long-lasting reminder of your event, milestone, or celebration
- Provide a keepsake that inspires change in behavior and change in lives
- Deliver the ultimate "thank you" gift that remains on coffee tables and bookshelves
- Generate the "wow" factor

Books are thoughtful gifts that provide a genuine sentiment that other promotional items cannot express. They promote employee discussions and interaction, reinforce an event's meaning or location, and they make a lasting impression. Use your book to say "Thank You" and show people that you care.

FedTelligence is available in bulk quantities and in customized versions at special discounts for agency, corporate, institutional, and educational purposes. To learn more please contact our Special Sales team at:

1.866.775.1696 • sales@advantageww.com • www.AdvantageSpecialSales.com

CPSIA information can be obtained at www.ICGtesting.com
Printed in the USA
BVOW072316040912

299579BV00002B/4/P